yummy

yummy

desserts you can make in
5 to 30 minutes

Caroline Brewester

DUNCAN BAIRD PUBLISHERS

LONDON

yummy
Caroline Brewester

DEDICATION
For Dominic and Aurelia – you are both truly yummy.

ACKNOWLEDGEMENTS
Thank you to Dominic, Tutu and all of my friends who gleefully expanded their waistlines while tasting the recipes from this book and always asked for second helpings. Also a big thank you to Grace and Nicole for their hard work and unstinting belief in this project, to William, Bridget and Manisha for the gorgeous photographs and styling, and to Borra for her ongoing support.

First published in the United Kingdom and Ireland in 2010 by
Duncan Baird Publishers Ltd
Sixth Floor, Castle House
75–76 Wells Street
London W1T 3QH

Conceived, created and designed by Duncan Baird Publishers

Managing Editor: Grace Cheetham
Editor: Nicole Bator
Managing Designer: Manisha Patel
Studio photography: William Lingwood
Photography Assistant: Isobel Wield
Food Stylist: Bridget Sargeson
Assistant Food Stylist: Jack Sargeson
Prop Stylist: Rachel Jukes

British Library Cataloguing-in-Publication Data:
A CIP record for this book is available from the British Library

ISBN: 978-1-84483-939-1

10 9 8 7 6 5 4 3 2 1

Typeset in Variable
Colour reproduction by Bright Arts, Hong Kong
Printed in Singapore by Imago

Publisher's Note: While every care has been taken in compiling the recipes for this book, Duncan Baird Publishers, or any other persons who have been involved in working on this publication, cannot accept responsibility for any errors or omissions, inadvertent or not, that may be found in the recipes or text, nor for any problems that may arise as a result of preparing one of these recipes. If you are pregnant or breastfeeding or have any special dietary requirements or medical conditions, it is advisable to consult a medical professional before following any of the recipes contained in this book. Ill or elderly people, babies, young children and women who are pregnant or breastfeeding should avoid any recipes containing uncooked egg whites.

Notes on the recipes
Unless otherwise stated:
- All recipes serve 4
- Use medium eggs and fruit
- Use ripe fruit and fresh herbs
- Use unsalted butter
- Do not mix metric and imperial measurements
- 1 tsp = 5ml • 1 tbsp = 15ml • 1 cup = 250ml

contents

introduction

Who doesn't love dessert? Nothing beats something sweet and yummy at the end of a meal; something that tantalizes the taste buds and creates delightful memories not just for you, the cook, but for the people you feed as well. With so many daily demands on our time, it's tempting to settle for something 'easy' like a chocolate bar, ice cream or a few shop-bought cookies, but although these substitutes may be convenient, they just don't compare to the satisfaction of a homemade dessert. Creating something from scratch, with the occasional assistance of good-quality, ready-made ingredients, doesn't have to take a lot of time, either. As the carefully chosen recipes in this book show, it really is possible to produce delicious desserts, from storecupboard to plate, in 30 minutes or less. This book shows you how to brighten up mundane midweek meals with a lavish last course that can turn dinner into an extraordinary event. All you need are some basic ingredients and a few easy tricks – which I'm about to share with you.

One of the best starting points for quick desserts is fruit. Whether it's summer or winter, keeping an assortment of fruit to hand opens up a world of opportunity when you want to whip up a treat. Some of the quickest fruit-based desserts can also be the healthiest. Choose fruits that are in season. They will be at their peak of ripeness, sweetness and fragrance and bursting with so much flavour, they'll need very little added sugar. If you have fruits that have begun to overripen, using them in a quick dessert can resurrect them – they'll need hardly any cooking to reach the point of perfect tenderness. Use leftover berries as decoration or purée them into a sauce to enhance any dessert with colour, flavour and texture.

Hot desserts are always slightly special, as the mere act of switching on the oven implies a sense of thoughtfulness and effort, even if the preparation is rapid. Chilled packs of pastry, ready rolled and ready to use, mean that pies and tarts become a reality in mere moments. Cooking bases and crusts separately from fillings and then uniting them at the last minute can radically reduce baking times, or, easier still, you can serve the separate elements in a more modern, 'deconstructed' style. For simple, speedy sponge puddings, all you have to do is whirl together some eggs, butter, sugar and flour in a food processor to make a cake mixture, add your favourite flavours and then bake in individual ramekins. As a special final touch, crown these creations with some custard or liqueur-laced whipped cream.

If unexpected guests pop by, or you just have a sudden urge to splurge, some of the most creative confections can be made from storecupboard standbys. Keep to hand some nuts, dried fruit and mixed peel for chopping, and you're off to a good start. Chocolate chips are great because they save you the time it takes to chop a bar of chocolate into small pieces for melting. Steep a few raisins in rum for a sophisticated, adult affair; toast a few flakes of coconut for a tropical twist; or go to town with a luxuriously layered, cherry-capped Knickerbocker Glory (see page 76). Sweet, sticky extras, such as honey, maple syrup and caramel sauce, are perfect for drizzles and dips, or for rippling through cream and yogurt.

Shortbread biscuits and sponge fingers are storecupboard stars that you'll be happy to have to hand when the need for a quick dessert arises. They have a long shelf life and are great served alongside other desserts. Best of all, they really shine when towered with fruit and cream, or dipped, dunked or drenched in liqueur and layered into a tiramisù or trifle. Crushed or crumbled, they make a crunchy base for creamy cheesecakes and other treats, too. Varying the flavours according to any fruits you have around means that the options are almost limitless.

Another way to make spontaneous desserts easier to whip up is to keep a tub or two of ice cream in the freezer. A simple scoop is a perfect partner to pie, and everyone adores an ice cream sundae. Frozen berries are another frosty asset. They require no pre-preparation and can be elegantly enrobed in warm white chocolate sauce; whizzed to make an instant ice cream or sorbet; puréed and rippled into crème fraîche; or paired with pastry for pies, crumbles and tarts.

No matter how much time you spend making a dessert, it should always look good – if it looks good then it will taste good! A few seconds spent adding a swirl of sauce, a sprinkling of fine sugar or a hint of mint leaves will elevate your creation into something that looks truly special. For an instant touch of elegance, decorate your dessert with chocolate curls simply by dragging a vegetable peeler along the side of a chocolate bar. Even a simple smattering of cocoa powder or a light dusting of icing sugar will give a dessert a more polished presentation – or indulge your inner child and let rip with a rainbow of sugar sprinkles scattered over the top.

There's never too little time to whip up the perfect dessert, no matter what the occasion. Life is short. Make dessert fast!

mango-coconut sundaes (see page 12)

CHAPTER ONE

5-minute desserts

Five minutes may seem like too little time to make anything, but most kitchens are stocked with a few basics that can go a long way. Ripe fruits, frozen berries, sweet jams and cream, for example, can form the base of some super-fast desserts. Use an electric mixer to whip cream in a flash, then ripple it with sweet papaya purée and mango to make sensational Tropical Fools. For a restaurant-style dessert, try Iced Berries with Hot White Chocolate Sauce – simply match frozen berries with the easiest mixture of warm chocolate and cream and the ingredients will melt together in just a couple of minutes. When you want a warm dessert, cook up some Crisp Cinnamon Puffs for a real melt-in-the-mouth treat. These recipes prove that there's no such thing as too little time for dessert.

mango-coconut sundaes

Puréed mango makes a super-fast sauce for ice cream and is a great way to transform mangos, even slightly overripe ones, into a delicious treat.

500ml/17fl oz/2 cups coconut or vanilla ice cream
4 tbsp unsweetened desiccated coconut or dried coconut flakes
1 large mango
juice of 1 lime, plus extra to taste

1 Remove the ice cream from the freezer and leave to stand at room temperature to soften slightly. Put the coconut in a dry frying pan and toast over a very low heat, stirring occasionally, for 2–3 minutes until golden brown. Immediately transfer it to a plate, spread it out and set aside.

2 Meanwhile, cut the mango away from the stone and use a spoon to scoop the flesh into a blender, discarding the skin. Add the lime juice and blend for 1 minute until smooth. Add more lime juice to taste, if necessary.

3 Divide half of the ice cream into four sundae glasses or deep bowls and drizzle half of the mango purée over it. Divide the remaining ice cream into the glasses, then spoon the remaining sauce over it. Sprinkle with the coconut and serve immediately.

bubbly berries

This is a quick but indulgent way to serve summer raspberries. First you eat the fruit, then you can enjoy the fruit-infused fizz as an after-dinner drink.

juice of 1 1/2 small lemons
4 tbsp icing sugar
200g/7oz/scant 2 cups raspberries
400ml/14fl oz/1 2/3 cups medium white or rosé sparkling wine, chilled
4 mint or basil sprigs, to decorate
crisp biscuits, such as langues de chat or cantucci, to serve

1 Put the lemon juice and icing sugar in a small bowl and stir until the sugar has dissolved. Divide the raspberries into four tall glasses and spoon over the lemon syrup.

2 Add the wine and decorate with mint sprigs. Serve immediately, with crisp biscuits on the side.

watermelon with mint sugar

Mint-flavoured sugar adds a fresh note to watermelon, as well as a pleasing colour contrast.

1 Cut the watermelon into 4 wedges, then remove and discard the rind and cut the flesh into large chunks. Arrange the watermelon on four plates and set aside.

2 Put the mint and caster sugar in a small bowl and crush together, using the back of a spoon, for 1–2 minutes until all the oils have been released from the mint. (You can also do this in a mini-chopper or using a mortar and pestle, or on a chopping board using the flat side of a large knife.) Sprinkle the mint sugar over the watermelon and serve decorated with mint sprigs.

900g/2lb seedless watermelon
1 large handful of mint leaves, finely chopped
2 tbsp caster sugar
4 mint sprigs, to decorate

orange-honey salad with toasted almonds

Throughout the Mediterranean and Middle East, fragrant fruit salads, such as this one flavoured with a hint of cardamom, are popular desserts.

1 Using a small serrated knife, cut the peel and pith away from the oranges and discard. Slice the oranges on a lipped plate to catch and reserve the juice that comes out during slicing. Arrange the slices on four plates and dust them with the cardamom. Transfer the reserved juice to small bowl.

2 Add the honey to the juice and mix well, then drizzle the mixture over the oranges. Scatter with the toasted almonds and serve decorated with mint sprigs.

4 large oranges
a large pinch of ground cardamom
2 tbsp clear honey
2 tbsp toasted flaked almonds
4 mint sprigs, to decorate

seared pear with dolcelatte

Serve this quick, sophisticated dessert as an alternative to a cheese course.

sunflower oil, for greasing
1 large firm pear, halved, cored
   and cut into 12 thin slices
225g/8oz dolcelatte, or similar
   blue cheese, thinly sliced
2 tbsp clear honey

1 Grease a ridged cast-iron griddle pan or heavy-based frying pan and heat it over a high heat. Cook the pear slices for 1-1$\frac{1}{2}$ minutes on each side until browned. Remove the slices from the griddle and arrange them on four plates.
2 Arrange the dolcelatte slices alongside the pears, drizzle with the honey and serve warm.

▸ grilled peach melba

The classic combination of peach and raspberry is given a new twist here by quickly grilling the peaches. The warm fruit and cold ice cream and sauce make a lovely contrast.

500ml/17fl oz/2 cups vanilla
   ice cream
4 small peaches, halved and pitted
225g/8oz/scant 2 cups raspberries
2 tsp icing sugar, plus extra
   if needed
juice of $\frac{1}{2}$ lemon

1 Preheat the grill to high. Remove the ice cream from the freezer and leave to stand at room temperature to soften slightly. Put the peach halves on a baking sheet, cut-sides up.
2 Grill for 2-3 minutes until warmed through. Meanwhile, put the raspberries, icing sugar and lemon juice in a blender or food processor and blend until puréed. Taste and add more sugar, if necessary.
3 Transfer the grilled peaches to four plates and top each one with a scoop of ice cream. Top with the raspberry sauce and serve immediately.

iced berries with hot white chocolate sauce

The creamy hot chocolate sauce in this recipe combines perfectly with frozen berries.

350g/12oz/4 cups frozen mixed berries, such as blackberries, strawberries and raspberries

HOT WHITE CHOCOLATE SAUCE
100g/3½oz/heaped ½ cup white chocolate chips
125ml/4fl oz/½ cup double cream

1 Divide the berries into four heatproof glasses or bowls and leave to stand at room temperature while you make the sauce.
2 Put the chocolate chips and cream in a heatproof bowl and rest it over a pan of gently simmering water, making sure the bottom of the bowl does not touch the water. Heat, stirring occasionally, for 2–3 minutes until well blended and the chocolate has melted.
3 Transfer the sauce to a heatproof jug and serve immediately with the berries, allowing each guest to pour some of the hot sauce over the berries.

nectarines with maple cream

It's easy to transform basic ingredients like crème fraîche by accenting them with different flavours, such as the maple syrup used here.

200g/7oz/scant 1 cup crème fraîche
finely grated zest of 1 lemon
5 tbsp maple syrup
4 nectarines or peaches, halved, pitted and sliced
amaretti biscuits, to serve

1 Put the crème fraîche, lemon zest and 1 tablespoon of the maple syrup in a small bowl and stir well, then set aside.
2 Arrange the nectarines on four plates. Add a large dollop of the maple cream to each plate and drizzle with the remaining maple syrup. Serve with amaretti biscuits.

hot strawberries romanov

Warming the strawberries in this recipe helps to bring out their flavour and sweetness.

juice of 2 large oranges
4 tbsp caster sugar
5 tbsp orange-flavoured liqueur,
   such as Cointreau
450g/1lb strawberries, hulled and
   halved or quartered, if large
125ml/4fl oz/$\frac{1}{2}$ cup double cream
1 tsp icing sugar
mint leaves, to decorate

1 Put the orange juice, caster sugar and 4 tablespoons of the liqueur in a small saucepan. Bring to the boil, stirring constantly. Add the strawberries and boil for 30 seconds, then set aside.
2 Put the cream and icing sugar in a bowl and whip, using an electric mixer, until soft peaks form, then whisk in the remaining liqueur.
3 Spoon the strawberries and sauce into four bowls and top with the whipped cream. Decorate with mint leaves and serve warm.

charoset

This crunchy fruit salad, made with apples, dried fruit and nuts, is traditionally served for Jewish Passover meals, but it's delicious at any time of the year.

1 Put the apples, raisins and walnuts in a large bowl and set aside. In a separate bowl, whisk together the red wine, honey and cinnamon, if using, whisking until the honey dissolves.

2 Spoon the sauce over the fruit and nuts and toss well, making sure the apple is well coated to prevent discolouration. Divide into four bowls and serve topped with yogurt and drizzled with extra honey.

3 Granny Smith apples, quartered, cored and diced
85g/3oz/²/₃ cup raisins
85g/3oz/scant ³/₄ cup chopped walnuts
4 tbsp fruity red wine, such as Beaujolais
4 tbsp clear honey, plus extra, to serve
a pinch of cinnamon (optional)
Greek yogurt or crème fraîche, to serve

citrus-flavoured crème fraîche dip

Flavoured crème fraîche is lovely with fresh fruit. Vary the items to dip according to your tastes and the season.

1 Put the crème fraîche, icing sugar, citrus zests and orange juice in a bowl and mix well. Spoon the dip into a large ramekin or bowl and put it in the centre of a large serving plate or board.

2 Arrange the fruit and muffin pieces and the biscuits on the plate around the dip. Decorate with mint and serve with wooden skewers or small forks that can be used to spear the fruit and muffin pieces and dunk them in the dip.

200g/7oz/scant 1 cup crème fraîche
1 tbsp icing sugar
finely grated zest of 1 small lime
finely grated zest of 1 small lemon
finely grated zest of ¹/₂ small orange, plus 1 tbsp juice
1 large peach, halved, pitted and cut into bite-sized pieces
8 strawberries, hulled and halved or quartered, if large
1 large apple, quartered, cored and cut into bite-sized slices
1 large chocolate muffin or similar, cut into bite-sized pieces
8 gingernut biscuits
1 mint sprig, to decorate

fruity couscous

Couscous cooks quickly and can be sweetened with juice and fruits to make a delicious and unusual dessert.

150g/5¹/₂oz/heaped ³/₄ cup
   quick-cooking couscous
350ml/12fl oz/1¹/₂ cups
   apple juice
8 ready-to-eat dried apricots,
   roughly chopped
55g/2oz/¹/₂ cup sultanas
2 tbsp pine nuts
clear honey, to serve
natural yogurt, to serve

1 Put the couscous and apple juice in a saucepan and bring to the boil over a medium heat, stirring occasionally. Add the apricots and sultanas and boil for 1 minute.

2 Remove the pan from the heat, cover and leave to stand for 3 minutes, or until all of the liquid has been absorbed. Meanwhile, put the pine nuts in a dry frying pan and cook over a medium heat, stirring occasionally, for 2–3 minutes until golden brown. Uncover the couscous and immediately stir the pine nuts in with a fork, fluffing up the couscous as you stir.

3 Spoon the mixture into four bowls or, for a prettier presentation, pack it into four 200ml/7fl oz/scant 1-cup pudding moulds or ramekins and then turn out on to plates. Serve drizzled with honey and topped with dollops of yogurt.

▶ chocolate-dipped physalis

Exotic sharp-sweet physalis covered in dark chocolate make an elegant dessert.

85g/3oz/¹/₂ cup dark
   chocolate chips
15g/¹/₂oz butter
20 physalis

1 Line a baking sheet that will fit in your freezer with baking parchment. Put the chocolate chips and butter in a heatproof bowl and rest it over a pan of gently simmering water, making sure the bottom of the bowl does not touch the water. Heat, stirring occasionally, for 2–3 minutes until the chocolate and butter have melted. Remove the bowl from the heat.

2 Meanwhile, peel back the papery leaves surrounding the physalis fruit but do not remove them. Twist the leaves together just above the point where they join the fruit. Dip the physalis into the chocolate, lift them out and allow any excess to drip back into the bowl, then put them on the baking sheet to set.

3 If the chocolate is too runny, freeze the physalis for 1 minute to help it set. Peel the physalis away from the parchment, arrange on a plate and serve.

tropical fools

Soft tropical fruits are ideal for blending and pairing with cream to make rich, irresistible fools.

2 papayas, halved and deseeded
juice of 1 small lime
2 tbsp icing sugar
250ml/9fl oz/1 cup double cream
1 small mango, peeled, pitted
   and cut into bite-sized cubes
shortbread biscuits, to serve

1 Scoop the papaya flesh into a blender, add the lime juice and icing sugar and blend for 1–2 minutes until smooth.
2 In a large bowl, whip the cream, using an electric mixer, until stiff peaks form, then fold in the papaya purée.
3 Spoon the fool into four glasses and spoon the mango cubes over them. Serve with shortbread biscuits.

jewelled winter fruit salad

Tropical fruits, such as persimmon and pomegranate, create a stunningly attractive dessert when served together. Make sure to use only soft, ripe persimmons – hard, unripe ones have a bitter, tannic taste.

1 pomegranate
juice of 1 large clementine
1 tbsp icing sugar
2 large persimmons, halved
   and each half sliced into
   6 half-moons
4 mint sprigs, to decorate

1 Halve the pomegranate and, using a fork, remove the seeds on to a plate, then remove and discard any white pith. In a small bowl, mix together the clementine juice and icing sugar, stirring until the sugar has dissolved.
2 Arrange the persimmon slices on a plate and scatter the pomegranate seeds over them. Drizzle with the clementine syrup and serve decorated with mint sprigs.

lemon possets

Lemon posset is a delicious dessert made with lemons
and cream. This version is ready in double-quick time.

1 In a small bowl, mix together the lemon curd and lemon zest
   and juice. In another bowl, whip the cream, using an electric mixer,
   until soft peaks form, then fold in the lemon mixture until just
   combined, being careful not to overmix.
2 Spoon the lemon posset into four glasses and decorate with
   lemon slices. Serve with crisp biscuits, if desired.

4 tbsp lemon curd
finely grated zest of 1 lemon,
   plus 2 tbsp lemon juice
300ml/10^1/$_2$fl oz/scant 1^1/$_4$ cups
   double cream
thin lemon slices, to decorate
crisp biscuits, such as langues
   de chat or cigarettes russes,
   (optional) to serve

▶ virtually instant raspberry sorbet

Frozen raspberries can be blended into such a fabulous sorbet, you'll never want to buy shop-bought versions again.

450g/1lb/3²/₃ cups frozen raspberries
100g/3¹/₂oz/scant ¹/₂ cup caster sugar
2 tsp lemon juice
4 ready-made meringues, to serve

1 Put the raspberries and caster sugar in a food processor and blend for 1 minute, or until roughly chopped. Stop and scrape down the sides of the food processor bowl as necessary.
2 Add the lemon juice and 2 tablespoons water and blend for a further 1–2 minutes until smooth. You may need to stop and scrape down the sides of the bowl halfway through.
3 Immediately spoon the sorbet into four bowls or glasses and serve with meringues.

banana-raisin panini

Toasted banana sandwiches are brought into the realm of dessert with sweet-scented cinnamon-raisin bread.

8 small slices of cinnamon-raisin bread
2 small bananas, peeled and thinly sliced
30g/1oz butter, softened
clear honey, to serve
whipped cream, to serve

1 Preheat a ridged, cast-iron griddle or frying pan over a high heat or preheat the grill to high. Lay out 4 slices of the bread on a work surface and arrange the banana slices over them. Cover with the remaining slices of bread, then thinly butter both sides of each sandwich.
2 Put the sandwiches on the griddle and cook for 1 minute on each side until lightly toasted. If grilling the sandwiches, grill for 1–2 minutes on each side.
3 Cut the sandwiches in half diagonally and stack on four plates. Serve drizzled with honey and topped with whipped cream.

papaya with three-way lime

Papaya and lime bring out the best in each other in this
refreshing, low-fat dessert.

1 Remove the sorbet from the freezer and leave to stand at room
temperature to soften slightly. Peel the papaya quarters and cut
them into thin slices or bite-sized chunks.

2 Arrange the papaya slices on four plates, or spoon the chunks
into four glasses or bowls, then sprinkle with the lime juice.

3 Cut the pared zest into thin, needle-like shards. Top each portion
of papaya with 1 scoop of the sorbet and sprinkle with the zest.
Decorate with mint leaves and serve immediately.

250ml/9fl oz/1 cup lime sorbet
2 papayas, halved lengthways,
   deseeded and cut into quarters
juice and finely pared zest of
   1 large lime
mint leaves, to decorate

cinnamon-glazed grapefruit

A quickly grilled cinnamon crust adds warmth and sweetness
to simple grapefruit.

1 Preheat the grill to high and line a baking sheet with foil. Trim
away a small sliver of peel from the bottom of each grapefruit
half so that the halves will rest flat when you put them on the
baking sheet. Slip a small, serrated knife between the flesh and
skin of the grapefruit halves and cut around to loosen the flesh
from the skin slightly. Put the grapefruit on the baking sheet,
cut-sides up.

2 In a small bowl, mix together the brown sugar and cinnamon,
then sprinkle the mixture evenly over the grapefruit.

3 Grill for 2–3 minutes until the sugar has melted and is bubbling
slightly. Serve hot, with yogurt for spooning over.

2 large grapefruit, halved
   crossways
4 tbsp soft light brown sugar
1 tsp cinnamon
natural yogurt or whipped cream,
   to serve

5

5-minute desserts

ginger syllabub

Syllabub is a traditional English dessert made with cream and alcohol. The addition of fresh ginger gives this a modern twist.

4cm/1½in piece root ginger, peeled and grated
2 tbsp icing sugar
6 tbsp ginger wine, such as Stone's, or sweet sherry
300ml/10½fl oz/scant 1¼ cups double cream
2 pieces preserved or crystallized ginger, chopped
crisp biscuits, such as langues de chat or cigarettes russes, to serve

1 Put the ginger, icing sugar and ginger wine in a bowl and stir until the sugar has dissolved, then set aside.
2 In a large bowl, whip the cream, using an electric mixer, until soft peaks form, then whisk in the ginger mixture, being careful not to overmix.
3 Spoon the syllabub into four glasses or bowls and sprinkle the preserved ginger over the top. Serve with crisp biscuits.

affogato all'amaretto with biscotti

Affogato – ice cream 'drowned' in coffee – has to be one of Italy's best-loved fast desserts. Here it is enhanced with the almondy notes of amaretto and biscotti.

500ml/17fl oz/2 cups vanilla ice cream
6 biscotti biscuits
4 tbsp amaretto liqueur
185ml/6fl oz/¾ cup hot espresso-strength coffee
cocoa powder, to serve

1 Remove the ice cream from the freezer and leave to stand at room temperature to soften slightly. Meanwhile, put 2 of the biscotti in a small plastic bag and crush into crumbs, using a rolling pin, then set aside. In a small bowl, mix together the amaretto and coffee.
2 Divide the ice cream into four bowls or wide coffee cups. Spoon the hot coffee and liqueur mixture over the ice cream and sprinkle the biscotti crumbs over the top.
3 Dust with a little cocoa powder and serve immediately, with the remaining biscotti on the side.

coffee granita

Granita, a traditional Sicilian speciality, has bigger ice crystals than a sorbet. This delicious, ultra-quick version is made by blending ice cubes and coffee in a food processor.

1 Dissolve the coffee granules in 2 tablespoons boiling water and set aside. Put the cream in a bowl and whip, using an electric mixer, until soft peaks form, then set aside.

2 Put the ice cubes in a food processor and blend for 1 minute, or until coarsely crushed. Add the caster sugar and coffee and blend for 1–2 minutes until crunchy granules form. You may need to stop and scrape down the sides of the bowl halfway through.

3 Spoon the granita into four glasses or coffee cups and top with the whipped cream. Dust each granita with cocoa powder and serve immediately.

4 tsp instant coffee granules
125ml/4fl oz/$1/2$ cup double cream
680g/1lb 8oz/5 cups ice cubes
100g/$3^1/2$oz/scant $1/2$ cup caster sugar
cocoa powder, to serve

◄ coffee parfaits

For a quick dessert, these layered sundaes have plenty of contrasting textures and intense flavours.

1 Remove the ice cream from the freezer and leave to stand at room temperature to soften slightly. Put the cream, icing sugar and vanilla extract in a bowl and whip, using an electric mixer, until soft peaks form.

2 Divide half of the ice cream and then most of the cookie crumbs into four glasses or deep bowls, then top with the remaining ice cream.

3 Drizzle with the liqueur, then scatter with most of the remaining cookie crumbs and top with the whipped cream. Decorate with the chocolate coffee beans and the rest of the cookie crumbs and serve immediately.

500ml/17fl oz/2 cups coffee
  ice cream
125ml/4fl oz/$^1/_2$ cup double cream
$^1/_2$ tsp icing sugar
$^1/_2$ tsp vanilla extract
2 giant double chocolate chip
  cookies, crumbled
4 tbsp coffee-flavoured liqueur,
  such as Kahlúa
12 chocolate coffee beans,
  or 2 tbsp chopped dark
  chocolate, to decorate

caramel-pecan popcorn

Popping corn is fun and takes almost no time. Drizzling it with dulce de leche or caramel sauce makes a sweet and sticky end to a meal.

1 Line a baking sheet with baking parchment. Heat the oil in a large casserole or stockpot with a tight-fitting lid over a high heat. Add the corn, cover and cook, shaking the pan occasionally, for 2 minutes or until the popping sound stops.

2 Spread the popcorn out in a single layer on the baking sheet and leave to cool for 1 minute. Meanwhile, put the dulce de leche and cream in a small bowl and mix well.

3 Drizzle the sauce over the popcorn and sprinkle with the pecans. Serve informally, allowing everyone to help themselves.

2 tbsp sunflower oil
100g/3$^1/_2$oz/$^1/_2$ cup popping corn
6 tbsp dulce de leche or caramel
  sauce
3 tbsp double cream
55g/2oz/$^1/_2$ cup pecan halves,
  roughly chopped

caramel creams

Dulce de leche is a wonderful ingredient to keep in the storecupboard for making quick desserts. Here it's rippled with rich vanilla-accented mascarpone for a truly decadent treat.

250ml/9fl oz/1 cup double cream
225g/8oz/scant 1 cup mascarpone cheese
1 tsp vanilla extract
1 tsp icing sugar
4 tbsp dulce de leche or caramel sauce, plus extra to serve

1 Put the cream in a large bowl and whip, using an electric mixer, until soft peaks form. In a separate bowl, beat the mascarpone, vanilla extract and icing sugar until smooth (no need to clean the beaters first). Stir in one-quarter of the whipped cream to loosen the mascarpone mixture, then whisk in the remaining whipped cream until just combined.

2 Spoon the dulce de leche over the cream mixture and stir once or twice to ripple the caramel through the cream, being careful not to overmix. Spoon the cream into four glasses or ramekins and serve drizzled with extra dulce de leche.

crisp cinnamon puffs

A very fast fritter, these delicious little puffs are bursting with spicy-sweet goodness.

500ml/17fl oz/2 cups rapeseed oil, for deep-frying
1 tbsp icing sugar
$1/4$ tsp cinnamon
$1/2$ sheet of ready-rolled puff pastry, about 150g/5$1/2$oz
natural yogurt, to serve

1 Heat the oil in a large heavy-based saucepan or deep-fat fryer until it reaches 180°C/350°F and preheat the oven to 70°C/150°F/Gas $1/4$. Meanwhile, mix the icing sugar and cinnamon together in a small bowl and set aside. Cut the pastry into 16 x 4cm/1$1/2$in squares.

2 Working in batches to avoid overcrowding the pan, fry the pastry squares in the hot oil for 1 minute on each side until puffed and golden brown. Remove from the oil, using a slotted spoon, drain on kitchen paper and keep warm in the oven while you make the remaining puffs. Return the oil to the correct temperature before starting each batch.

3 Dust the puffs with the cinnamon sugar, then turn them over and dust again. Serve warm with yogurt for dipping.

cannoli cream pots

The ricotta cream filling used in traditional Italian cannoli is quick to make and can be served as a dessert on its own. If you have extra time, serve these in the Brandy Snap Baskets on page 83.

1 Put the chocolate chips in a heatproof bowl and rest it over a pan of gently simmering water, making sure the bottom of the bowl does not touch the water. Heat, stirring occasionally, for 2–3 minutes until the chocolate has melted. Remove the bowl from the heat.

2 Meanwhile, in a large bowl, beat the ricotta and cream, using an electric mixer, for 1 minute until smooth. Beat in the vanilla extract, icing sugar and liqueur, if using, then stir in the mixed peel and orange zest.

3 Divide the ricotta mixture into four ramekins or small glasses. Spoon the melted chocolate over the top and sprinkle with the pistachios. Serve with crisp biscuits, if desired.

4 tbsp dark chocolate chips
350g/12oz/scant 1½ cups ricotta cheese, drained
2 tbsp double cream
1 tsp vanilla extract
1 tbsp icing sugar
1 tbsp orange-flavoured liqueur, such as Cointreau (optional)
40g/1½oz/scant ⅓ cup chopped mixed peel
finely grated zest of 1 large orange
2 tbsp shelled unsalted pistachios, coarsely chopped, to decorate
crisp biscuits, such as brandy snaps (optional), to serve

yogurt & cassis ripple (see page 36)

CHAPTER TWO

10-minute desserts

Ten minutes gives you time for a little extra preparation and the chance to add pizzazz to your desserts. All you have to do is melt some sugar, stir in some cream and you've got a gorgeous home-made toffee sauce to drizzle over bananas, meringues and whipped cream for a delightful Banoffee Pavlova. When you want to really indulge in something special, go for Tipsy Ten-Minute Tiramisù – layers of rich mascarpone, Marsala-soused sponge fingers and chopped chocolate make this a knock-out dessert with adult flare. Or impress everyone with fruity Fast Berry Ice Cream, which comes together in the blink of an eye using a food processor. These and the other recipes here prove just how easy it is to turn quick desserts into something magical.

yogurt & cassis ripple

Crème de cassis elevates yogurt into a quick dessert and adds a gorgeous splash of colour.

175g/6oz/²/₃ cup blackcurrant or blackberry yogurt
3 tbsp crème de cassis liqueur, plus extra to serve
250ml/9fl oz/1 cup double cream
1 tsp vanilla extract
1 tsp icing sugar
250g/9oz/1 cup Greek yogurt
1-2 squares of white chocolate, to serve
crisp biscuits, such as langues de chat or cigarettes russes, to serve

1 Put the blackcurrant yogurt and crème de cassis in a large bowl and mix well, then set aside. Put the cream, vanilla extract and icing sugar in a separate bowl and whip, using an electric mixer, until soft peaks form, then fold in the Greek yogurt. Spoon this mixture over the blackcurrant yogurt and stir once or twice to ripple the two mixtures. Be careful not to overmix.

2 Spoon the ripple into four glasses or bowls. Drizzle a little extra cassis into the glasses and grate the white chocolate over the tops. Serve with crisp biscuits on the side.

strawberry shortbread stacks

Crisp shortbread biscuits layered with cream and strawberries make an irresistible summer dessert.

225g/8oz small strawberries, hulled and halved or thickly sliced, plus 4 whole small strawberries, reserved, to decorate
2 tsp icing sugar, plus extra, to serve
1 tbsp brandy (optional)
250ml/9fl oz/1 cup double cream
¹/₄ tsp vanilla extract
8 round, thin shortbread biscuits

1 Put the strawberries, 1 teaspoon of the icing sugar and the brandy, if using, in a bowl. If omitting the brandy, add 1 table-spoon water. Toss together, then leave to stand for 2 minutes.

2 Meanwhile, put the cream, vanilla extract and remaining icing sugar in a large bowl and whip, using an electric mixer, until soft peaks form. Drain the liquid from the strawberries into the whipped cream and fold together.

3 Put 1 biscuit on each of four plates and top with half of the strawberries. Top with half of the whipped cream, then add the remaining strawberries. Cover with the remaining shortbread biscuits and crown each stack with a spoonful of the cream. Serve decorated with the reserved strawberries and dusted with icing sugar.

stuffed dates

This quick sweetmeat, flavoured with ground almonds and
a hint of orange, is popular in Morocco.

1 Put the almonds and icing sugar in a small bowl and stir well. Add
the orange flower water a few drops at a time, stirring until the
almonds and sugar hold together and form a somewhat dry paste.
You may not need all of the liquid.

2 Divide the paste into 12 equal portions and roll them into small
logs. Open out the dates and put one piece of the almond paste
in the centre of each one, where the pit was, then push the sides
of the date together to enclose the paste. Arrange the dates on
a serving plate and serve dusted with icing sugar.

30g/1oz/$^1/_3$ cup ground almonds
3 tbsp icing sugar, plus extra
   to serve
1 tsp orange flower water
   or orange juice
12 pitted dates, split lengthways

mango & melon with mojito syrup

Lime, mint and rum syrup – the flavours in the popular mojito
cocktail – are used here to transform a fresh fruit salad into
an exotic treat.

1 To make the syrup, put the mint and icing sugar in a small bowl
and crush together, using the back of a spoon, for 1–2 minutes
until the oils have been released from the mint. (You can also
do this in a mini-chopper or using a mortar and pestle, or on
a chopping board, using the flat side of a large knife.) Stir in the
rum, lime juice and 2 tablespoons water, then pour the mixture
into a bowl, scraping out any mint that sticks to the bottom
of the bowl. Add the mango and set aside.

2 Remove the rind from the melon quarters and cut the flesh into
bite-sized chunks, then add them to the syrup.

3 Gently toss together the fruit and syrup and spoon the mixture
into four glasses or bowls. Serve decorated with mint sprigs.

mint leaves from 4 large mint
   sprigs, plus 4 mint sprigs
   for decoration
4 tbsp icing sugar
2 tbsp white rum
juice of 1 large lime
1 large mango, peeled, pitted and
   chopped into bite-sized pieces
1 green melon, such as galia,
   cut into quarters and deseeded

strawberry bruschetta

Bruschetta is usually served at the start of a meal and covered with savoury toppings, but this sweet twist is a great way to end a meal. A slightly stale loaf of bread is ideal for this recipe.

1 Preheat the grill to high. Toast the bread on both sides, then spread a thin layer of the chocolate-hazelnut spread over one side of each slice and put them, spread-sides up, on a baking sheet.

2 Divide the strawberries over the spread and grill for 1 minute, or until the strawberries are just warm. Dust with icing sugar and serve hot.

1 loaf of ciabatta, preferably 1 day old, cut into 8 or 12 slices, each about 1cm/$\frac{1}{2}$in thick
4 tbsp chocolate-hazelnut spread
350g/12oz strawberries, hulled and thickly sliced
1 tsp icing sugar, to serve

honey-flavoured waffles with hot plums

Frozen waffles make a crisp and delicious base for warm plums when they are grilled and flavoured with honey.

1 Preheat the grill to high and preheat a ridged, cast-iron griddle pan or heavy-based frying pan over a medium heat. Put the plums in the pan, cut-sides down, and cook for 1–2 minutes, turning once, until warmed through, then set aside, covered, to keep warm.

2 Put the waffles on a grill pan and brush the tops with a little of the melted butter. Grill for 1–2 minutes until golden and crisp, then turn them over, brush with the remaining butter and grill for a further 1–2 minutes. Drizzle 2 tablespoons of the honey over the waffles and grill for a further 1 minute, or until the honey bubbles slightly.

3 Transfer the waffles to plates and top with the plums. Drizzle with the remaining honey and serve hot with whipped cream.

4 large firm plums, quartered and pitted
4 large frozen waffles
1 tbsp melted butter
6 tbsp clear honey
whipped cream or vanilla ice cream, to serve

grilled figs with cheese & honey

Aromatic cardamom-scented honey lifts the sweet/sharp flavour combination of figs and goat's cheese to a new level.

seeds from 4 cardamom pods,
    lightly crushed
6 tbsp clear honey
4 large or 8 small figs,
    halved lengthways
1 tsp icing sugar
115g/4oz log fresh goat's cheese,
    cut into 4 slices

1 Preheat the grill to high and line a grill pan with foil. Meanwhile, put the cardamom seeds, honey and 1 tablespoon water in a small saucepan and bring to the boil over a high heat, stirring. Leave to bubble for 30 seconds, then remove from the heat and set aside to infuse.

2 Put the figs on the grill pan, cut-sides up, and dust with the icing sugar. Put the pan as close as possible to the heat source and grill for 3 minutes or until the sugar bubbles and the figs soften slightly. Meanwhile, divide the cheese on to four plates.

3 Top the cheese with the figs and spoon the cardamom-infused honey, including the seeds, over them. Serve immediately.

grilled navel oranges with vanilla crusts

Vanilla sugar is very quick and easy to prepare, and it makes an aromatic crust for sweet navel oranges.

4 large navel oranges, cut in half
    horizontally
4 tbsp orange-flavoured liqueur,
    such as Cointreau (optional)
15g/1/2oz butter, chilled
crème fraîche, to serve

VANILLA SUGAR:
1/2 vanilla pod, cut into 4 pieces
4 tbsp caster sugar

1 Preheat the grill to high and line a baking sheet with foil. To make the vanilla sugar, put the vanilla pod pieces in a food processor or mini chopper and pulse 3 or 4 times to chop. Add the caster sugar and blend for 1 minute until well combined and the vanilla pod is finely chopped, then set aside.

2 Put the orange halves on the baking sheet, cut-sides up, trimming away a small sliver of peel from the bottom of each one so that they rest flat. Sprinkle with the liqueur, if using, then sprinkle evenly with the vanilla sugar. Cut the butter into four equal pieces and put 1 piece on top of each orange half.

3 Grill for 7–8 minutes until the sugar is bubbling, then serve hot with crème fraîche for spooning over.

fast berry ice cream

This is the fastest, freshest and most flavourful ice cream you will ever taste!

125ml/4fl oz/$\frac{1}{2}$ cup double cream
350g/12oz/4 cups frozen mixed berries
4 tbsp caster sugar
crisp biscuits, such as cigarettes russes, to serve

1 Put the cream in a medium bowl and whip, using an electric mixer, until soft peaks form, then set aside. Put the berries and caster sugar in a food processor and blend for 1–2 minutes until the mixture looks like large crystals. Stop and scrape down the sides of the food processor bowl as necessary.

2 Add the cream and blend for a further 2 minutes until smooth. You may need to stop and scrape down the sides of the bowl halfway through. Immediately spoon the ice cream into four bowls or glasses and serve with crisp biscuits.

apricot & amaretto creams

Apricots have a slightly almond flavour, so this indulgent amaretto-flavoured cream is a perfect accompaniment to the succulent summer fruit.

1 Preheat the grill to high. Put the cream, icing sugar and vanilla extract in a medium bowl and whip, using an electric mixer, until soft peaks form. Add the amaretto and whisk until just combined. Be careful not to overmix.

2 Put the apricots on a baking sheet, cut-sides down, and grill for 1 minute. Turn the apricots over and grill for a further 1–2 minutes until they are warmed through.

3 Divide the apricots on to four plates and top with the cream. Sprinkle with flaked almonds and serve.

125ml/4fl oz/^{1}/$_2$ cup double cream
2 tsp icing sugar
^{1}/$_4$ tsp vanilla extract
2 tbsp amaretto liqueur
4 large or 8 small apricots, halved and pitted
1 tbsp flaked almonds, to serve

bananas foster

Flambéeing, or flaming, is an impressive way to make a dessert really stand out – and it's easier than you might think.

1 Melt the butter in a 30cm/12in heavy-based frying pan over a medium heat. Add the brown sugar and cook, stirring, for 2 minutes, or until the sugar has melted, then add the nutmeg. Bring to the boil and boil for 2 minutes until the sugar has darkened slightly.

2 Add the bananas and cook for 1 minute, then turn them over and cook for a further 1–2 minutes until they have softened. Remove the pan from the heat and set aside.

3 Put the rum in a small saucepan over a medium heat until warm, then carefully ignite it with a match and pour it over the bananas, pouring away from you. Allow the alcohol to burn off and the flame to extinguish itself. (Alternatively, boil the rum for 1–2 minutes until the alcohol has evaporated and pour it over the bananas.)

4 Divide the bananas on to four plates and drizzle the sauce over them. Leave to cool slightly, then serve with whipped cream.

55g/2oz butter
4 tbsp soft light brown sugar
^{1}/$_4$ tsp freshly grated nutmeg, plus extra to serve
4 slightly underripe bananas, peeled and cut in half lengthways
4 tbsp dark rum
whipped cream, to serve

▶raspberry & hazelnut eton mess

Eton Mess is a divine, traditional English combination of cream, strawberries and crushed meringues. This take on the classic is made with raspberries – and whips up in almost no time at all.

4 tbsp chopped hazelnuts
115g/4oz/scant 1 cup raspberries
4 tbsp hazelnut-flavoured liqueur, such as Frangelico (optional)
250ml/9fl oz/1 cup double cream
$1/4$ tsp vanilla extract
2 ready-made meringue nests or 4 meringues, broken into small pieces

1 Put the hazelnuts in a dry frying pan and cook over a medium heat, stirring frequently, for 2–3 minutes until lightly browned. Immediately transfer to a plate and set aside to cool slightly.

2 Reserve 4 of the raspberries for decoration and put the rest in a bowl. Add the liqueur, if using, and crush lightly with a fork.

3 Put the cream and vanilla extract in a large bowl and whip, using an electric mixer, until soft peaks form. Fold the raspberry mixture and meringues into the cream, then spoon the mixture into four glasses or bowls. Scatter the toasted hazelnuts over the top, decorate with the reserved raspberries and serve.

sweet & sour strawberries with white chocolate cream

Strawberries and balsamic vinegar are delicious together – and especially pleasing with a white chocolate cream.

4 tbsp balsamic vinegar
2 tbsp soft light brown sugar
150ml/5fl oz/scant $2/3$ cup double cream
55g/2oz white chocolate, finely grated
450g/1lb small strawberries, hulled

1 Put the balsamic vinegar, brown sugar and 2 tablespoons water in a small saucepan and cook over a high heat, stirring, for 2 minutes until the sugar has dissolved. Bring to the boil and boil for 1–2 minutes, or until syrupy. Remove the pan from the heat, pour the syrup into a large heatproof bowl and set aside to cool slightly.

2 Meanwhile, put the cream in a medium bowl and whip, using an electric mixer, until soft peaks form, then fold in the chocolate.

3 Gently stir the strawberries into the balsamic syrup, then spoon the mixture into four glasses or bowls. Drizzle any syrup left in the bowl over the mixture and serve warm with the white chocolate cream.

insalata di sicily

Sicily is famous for its wonderful fruit, particularly lemons, which flavour the renowned limoncello liqueur used here. It adds a delicious, tart/sweet dimension to whipped cream.

150ml/5fl oz/scant $^2/_3$ cup
  double cream
1 tbsp icing sugar
finely grated zest of $^1/_2$ lemon
2 tbsp limoncello liqueur
225g/8oz/heaped 1 cup cherries,
  pitted and stems removed
225g/8oz/1$^1/_2$ cups strawberries,
  hulled and halved or quartered,
  if large
2 large peaches, preferably white,
  halved, pitted and each half
  cut into 8 slices
4 mint sprigs, to decorate

1 Put the cream, icing sugar and lemon zest in a bowl and whip, using an electric mixer, until soft peaks form. Add the limoncello and whisk until just combined.

2 Spoon the limoncello cream into four bowls and arrange the cherries, strawberries and peaches over it. Serve decorated with mint sprigs.

grape compôte

Demerara sugar's caramel tones make a flavourful syrup that complements the freshness of the grapes in this easy treat.

1 Put the demerara sugar, sherry, if using, and 125ml/4fl oz/$\frac{1}{2}$ cup water in a large saucepan and cook over a medium heat for 1–2 minutes, stirring occasionally, until the sugar has dissolved. Bring to the boil over a high heat and boil for 4 minutes, or until syrupy.

2 Drop the grapes into the hot syrup and leave to bubble for a few seconds, then remove the pan from the heat.

3 Spoon the grapes into four heatproof bowls or glasses and pour the syrup over them. Serve topped with whipped cream and sprinkled with a little extra sugar.

85g/3oz/heaped $\frac{1}{3}$ cup demerara sugar, plus extra to serve
2 tbsp sherry (optional)
225g/8oz seedless red grapes
225g/8oz seedless green grapes
whipped cream, to serve

berry banana splits

The fresh berry sauce in this banana split is a healthier and more colourful alternative to the usual chocolate sauce.

1 Remove the ice cream from the freezer and leave to stand at room temperature to soften slightly. Meanwhile, put the almonds in a dry frying pan and cook over a medium heat, stirring frequently, for 3–4 minutes until lightly browned. Immediately transfer them to a plate and set aside to cool slightly.

2 Put the strawberries, blueberries, raspberries, icing sugar and lemon juice in a blender or food processor and blend for 1–2 minutes until puréed. Pass the purée through a fine sieve into a clean bowl to remove the seeds.

3 Peel the bananas, then cut them in half lengthways and put them in four large bowls or on oval plates. Top each portion of bananas with 2 scoops of ice cream, then spoon the berry sauce over the top. Sprinkle with the almonds and serve.

500ml/17fl oz/2 cups strawberry or vanilla ice cream
2 tbsp flaked almonds
4 large strawberries, hulled
55g/2oz/$\frac{1}{3}$ cup blueberries
55g/2oz/heaped $\frac{1}{3}$ cup raspberries
2 tbsp icing sugar
1$\frac{1}{2}$ tsp lemon juice
4 bananas

▸rosewater & berry ripples

Fragrant rosewater gives this slightly unusual rippled dessert a distinctive floral flavour.

8 large strawberries, hulled
55g/2oz/heaped 1/3 cup
   raspberries
2 tbsp caster sugar
1 tbsp rosewater
250ml/9fl oz/1 cup double cream
2 tsp icing sugar
1 tsp vanilla extract
175g/6oz/3/4 cup Greek yogurt
4 pieces rosewater-flavoured
   Turkish delight, chopped,
   to decorate

1 Put the strawberries, raspberries, caster sugar and rosewater in a blender or food processor and blend for 1–2 minutes until puréed. Rub the purée through a fine sieve to remove the seeds and set aside.

2 Put the cream, icing sugar and vanilla extract in a large bowl and, using an electric mixer, whip until stiff peaks form. Fold in the yogurt, then spoon the purée over the mixture and stir once or twice to ripple through slightly. Be careful not to overmix.

3 Spoon the mixture into four glasses or bowls and serve decorated with the Turkish delight.

cherry fools

Tinned cherries are a wonderful standby to have to hand for quick desserts. In this recipe, they are easily transformed into a creamy fool.

450g/1lb tinned pitted black
   cherries in syrup, strained,
   with syrup reserved
150g/51/2oz/scant 2/3 cup
   cherry yogurt
2 tbsp kirsch liqueur (optional)
250ml/9fl oz/1 cup double cream
1 or 2 drops of almond extract,
   to taste
flaked almonds, preferably
   toasted, to decorate
shortbread biscuits, to serve

1 Put 115g/4oz/heaped 1/2 cup of the cherries in a blender and add the yogurt and kirsch, if using. Blend for 1–2 minutes until smooth.

2 Put the cream and almond extract in a large bowl and whip, using an electric mixer, until stiff peaks form. Fold the cherry mixture into the cream.

3 Reserve 4 of the remaining cherries for decoration and divide the rest into four glasses or bowls. Top with the cream mixture and then drizzle 1 tablespoon of the reserved syrup over each of the fools. Decorate with the reserved cherries and almonds. Serve with shortbread biscuits.

◄ kiwi fools

Kiwi fruit are pretty when sliced, and their bright, tart flavour
cuts through the richness of the cream in this fool.

1 Thinly slice 1 kiwi fruit and set aside. Chop the remaining kiwi fruit
   into chunks, put them in a blender and blend for 1–2 minutes until
   puréed. Add the honey and blend until just mixed.
2 Put the cream in a large bowl and whip, using an electric mixer,
   until stiff peaks form. Fold in the kiwi fruit purée, then spoon the
   mixture into four small glasses or bowls. Top with the reserved
   kiwi fruit slices and serve with crisp biscuits, if desired.

5 large kiwi fruit, peeled
4 tbsp clear honey
250ml/9fl oz/1 cup double cream
crisp biscuits, such as shortbread
  or ginger snaps, (optional) to
  serve

griddled apples with cinnamon croûtons

This easy, deconstructed version of apple charlotte comes
together in minutes to make a fabulous dessert.

1 Remove the ice cream from the freezer and leave to stand
   at room temperature to soften slightly. Preheat a large, ridged,
   cast-iron griddle pan or heavy-based frying pan over a high heat.
   Trim thin slices from the top and bottom of each apple, then cut
   each one crossways into 4 slices. Remove the core from the
   centre of each slice, using an apple corer or small, sharp knife.
2 Cut out 2 circles from each slice of bread, using a 5cm/2in round
   biscuit cutter. Mix the caster sugar and cinnamon together on a
   plate and set aside.
3 Put the apple slices in the griddle pan and cook, pressing down
   firmly, for 3 minutes on each side, or until softened. Meanwhile,
   melt half of the butter in a large frying pan over a medium heat.
   When it is foaming and slightly brown, add the bread slices and
   fry for 1–2 minutes until golden brown. Turn the slices over, add
   the remaining butter to the pan and continue frying for a further
   1 minute, or until golden and crisp.
4 Transfer the croûtons to the plate with the cinnamon sugar and
   press down so that the sugar sticks to the surface. Put 2 apple
   slices on each of four plates and top each portion with 2 coated
   croûtons. Serve with the ice cream on the side.

250ml/9fl oz/1 cup vanilla ice
  cream, to serve
2 large eating apples, such as royal
  gala or braeburn
4 slices of white bread, preferably
  slightly stale
4 tbsp caster sugar
1 tbsp cinnamon
30g/1oz butter

10

bananas in coconut cream

For a quick, Asian-inspired treat, try this popular dessert from Thailand.

1/2 tsp cornflour
400ml/14fl oz/1²/₃ cups coconut milk
1 tbsp caster sugar, plus extra to serve
4 slightly underripe bananas, peeled and halved lengthways
finely grated zest of 1 small lime, to serve

1 Put the cornflour and 1 tablespoon water in a small bowl and stir until smooth. Put the coconut milk and caster sugar in a large saucepan and bring to the boil over a medium heat. Add the cornflour paste and boil, whisking continuously, for 1–2 minutes until the milk thickens slightly.

2 Reduce the heat to low, add the bananas and cook very gently for 4 minutes, or until the bananas are tender. Do not stir, as the bananas might break up.

3 Carefully spoon the bananas into four bowls and spoon the coconut cream over them. Sprinkle with a little lime zest and serve warm with extra sugar alongside so that everyone can sweeten the coconut cream to taste.

mango, blood orange & basil salad

Herbs aren't often featured in desserts, but this recipe shows how they can brighten up something as simple as a fruit salad.

4 large basil sprigs
4 tbsp caster sugar
4 large blood oranges
1 large or 2 medium mangos

1 Remove the tips and smaller leaves from the basil sprigs and set aside. Put the remaining leaves and stems, the caster sugar and 4 tablespoons water in a saucepan and cook over a high heat, stirring, for 2–3 minutes until the sugar has dissolved. Bring to the boil and boil for 3 minutes until syrupy. Remove from the heat and set aside to cool while you prepare the fruit.

2 Cut the peel and pith away from the oranges, using a small serrated knife, then cut the oranges into segments and set aside in a bowl. Peel the mango and cut the flesh away from the pit in long slices. Arrange the fruit on four plates or in glasses.

3 Strain the basil syrup through a sieve into a clean bowl and spoon it over the fruit. Serve decorated with the reserved basil leaves.

banoffee pavlova

Banana, caramel and ready-made meringues combine in a lovely pavlova that is great for all seasons.

1 Put the caster sugar and 2 tablespoons water in a saucepan and cook over a medium heat, stirring, for 30 seconds–1 minute or until the sugar has dissolved. Bring to the boil over a high heat and boil for 4–5 minutes until the syrup has turned a medium caramel colour. Remove from the heat and stir in 6 tablespoons of the cream, being very careful as it may sputter a bit.

2 Return the pan to a low heat and cook, stirring, for 1–2 minutes until any hard lumps of caramel have dissolved, then keep warm over a very low heat.

3 Put the remaining cream in a large bowl and whip, using an electric mixer, until soft peaks form. Peel and slice the bananas.

4 Put the meringue nests on four plates and spoon the whipped cream over them. Top with the banana slices, drizzle with the sauce and serve. Alternatively, crumble the meringues into four glasses, layer with cream, bananas and sauce and serve.

85g/3oz/¹⁄₃ cup caster sugar
250ml/9fl oz/1 cup double cream
2 large bananas
4 ready-made meringue nests
   or 8 small meringues

tipsy ten-minute tiramisù

This egg-free version of tiramisù is made more decadent with the addition of creamy Irish whiskey.

2 tsp instant coffee granules
2 tbsp Marsala wine
50g/2oz/$\frac{1}{4}$ cup dark chocolate chips
225g/8oz/scant 1 cup mascarpone cheese
4 tbsp Irish cream whiskey, such as Baileys
2 tbsp icing sugar
250ml/9fl oz/1 cup double cream
$\frac{1}{2}$ tsp vanilla extract
8 sponge finger biscuits, each broken into 3 pieces
1 tsp cocoa powder, to serve

1 Put the coffee and 100ml/3$\frac{1}{2}$fl oz/scant $\frac{1}{2}$ cup water in a shallow bowl and mix until dissolved, then stir in the Marsala wine and set aside. Put the chocolate chips in a food processor and pulse until finely chopped.

2 Put the mascarpone, Irish cream and icing sugar in a large bowl and beat, using an electric mixer, for 1 minute until combined. Put the cream and vanilla extract in another bowl and whip until soft peaks form (no need to clean the beaters first), then fold it into the mascarpone mixture.

3 Dip half of the biscuit pieces in the coffee mixture and arrange them in the base of four glasses or bowls. Spoon half of the chocolate, then half of the mascarpone mixture, over the biscuits. Dip the remaining biscuit pieces in the coffee and layer again with the remaining chocolate and mascarpone. Serve dusted with the cocoa powder.

raspberries with marsala mascarpone

Tart raspberries and sweet Marsala wine prove a perfect combination in this delicious, creamy concoction.

350g/12oz/2$\frac{3}{4}$ cups raspberries
4 tbsp Marsala wine
4 tbsp icing sugar
225g/8oz/scant 1 cup mascarpone cheese
4 tbsp double cream
4 mint sprigs, to decorate
crisp biscuits, such as amaretti or cantuccini, to serve

1 Reserve 20 of the plumpest raspberries for decoration. Put half of the remaining raspberries in a bowl and crush lightly with a fork. Stir in the rest of the raspberries and the Marsala wine and icing sugar. Leave to stand for 5 minutes.

2 Meanwhile, put the mascarpone and cream in a bowl and beat, using an electric mixer, until just smooth. Strain any liquid from the raspberries into a small bowl and stir half of it into the mascarpone mixture along with the raspberries.

3 Spoon the mascarpone mixture into four glasses or bowls and spoon the remaining liquid over them. Decorate with the reserved raspberries and mint sprigs, then serve with crisp biscuits.

tofu-chocolate puddings

This rich pudding has such a wonderful, creamy texture it's hard to believe it's dairy-free!

SERVES 4-6
175g/6oz/1 cup dark chocolate chips
450g/1lb silken tofu, drained
4 tbsp icing sugar
1 tsp vanilla extract
4 or 6 mint sprigs, to decorate

1 Put four 240ml/8oz/scant 1-cup or six 150ml/5oz/scant $^2/_3$-cup freezerproof glasses or bowls in the freezer to chill. Put the chocolate chips in a heatproof bowl and rest it over a pan of gently simmering water, making sure the bottom of the bowl does not touch the water. Heat for 2-3 minutes, stirring occasionally, until the chocolate has melted. Remove the bowl from the heat.

2 Meanwhile, blot the tofu dry with plenty of kitchen paper, then transfer it to a blender. Add the icing sugar and vanilla extract and blend for 1 minute until smooth. Add the melted chocolate and blend again until just combined.

3 Spoon the pudding into the chilled glasses and freeze for 5 minutes to firm up the texture slightly. Serve decorated with mint sprigs.

rum & raisin sundaes

Rum and raisin sauce is a classic favourite and with good reason – it is quick to make and a perfect addition to ice cream sundaes.

500ml/17fl oz/2 cups vanilla ice cream
$^1/_2$ pineapple, peeled, cored and cut crossways into 4 x 1cm/$^1/_2$ in-thick rings

RUM & RAISIN SAUCE:
55g/2oz/scant $^1/_2$ cup raisins
125ml/4fl oz/$^1/_2$ cup gold or dark rum
55g/2oz/$^1/_4$ cup caster sugar
4 tbsp double cream

1 Remove the ice cream from the freezer and leave to stand at room temperature to soften slightly. To make the sauce, put the raisins, rum, caster sugar and 125ml/4fl oz/$^1/_2$ cup water in a saucepan and cook over a medium heat, stirring, for 3-4 minutes until the sugar has dissolved. Bring to the boil over a high heat and boil for 1-2 minutes until syrupy, then remove from the heat and leave to stand for 5 minutes.

2 Meanwhile, put 1 pineapple ring in each of four bowls or on plates. Top each one with a large scoop of ice cream.

3 Stir the cream into the rum and raisin sauce and spoon it over the ice cream and fruit. Serve immediately.

10-minute desserts

chocolate-coconut ice cream sandwiches

You can easily transform shop-bought biscuits into a treat that dessert lovers of all ages will adore.

1 Remove the ice cream from the freezer and leave to stand at room temperature to soften slightly. Put the chocolate chips in a heatproof bowl and rest it over a pan of gently simmering water, making sure the bottom of the bowl does not touch the water. Heat, stirring occasionally, for 2–3 minutes until the chocolate has melted. Remove the bowl from the heat.

2 Spread the melted chocolate over the top of each biscuit and sprinkle with the coconut. Put the biscuits, chocolate-sides up, on a small baking sheet or a plate and freeze for 5 minutes until the chocolate has set.

3 Turn 4 of the chocolate-coated biscuits over and put a scoop of the ice cream on each one, then sandwich with the remaining biscuits, chocolate-sides up. Serve immediately.

500ml/17fl oz/2 cups coconut or vanilla ice cream
175g/6oz/1 cup dark chocolate chips
8 digestive biscuits
4 tbsp unsweetened desiccated coconut

filo ribbons

Fried filo pastry makes a whimsical dessert. Here, it's absolutely delicious served with honey, pine nuts and ice cream.

250ml/9fl oz/1 cup vanilla
   ice cream
500ml/17fl oz/2 cups rapeseed oil,
   for deep-frying
4 tbsp pine nuts
2 sheets of filo pastry
4 tbsp clear honey
4 mint sprigs, to decorate

1 Remove the ice cream from the freezer and leave to stand at room temperature to soften slightly. Heat the oil in a deep heavy-based saucepan or deep-fat fryer until it reaches 180°C/350°F. Meanwhile, put the pine nuts in a dry frying pan and cook over a medium heat, stirring frequently, for 2–3 minutes until lightly browned and toasted. Immediately transfer them to a plate and set aside to cool slightly.

2 Roll up the filo sheets lengthways and cut, from the short end, into 5mm/1/4in-thick slices. Shake the slices open so they look like ribbons. Working in batches to avoid overcrowding the pan, drop 1 handful of the filo ribbons into the oil and deep-fry for 1 1/2 minutes until golden. Remove from the oil, using a slotted spoon, and drain on kitchen paper.

3 Divide the filo ribbons on to four plates and top each portion with 1 scoop of ice cream. Sprinkle with the pine nuts and drizzle with the honey. Decorate with mint sprigs and serve immediately.

coppa di zuccotto

Zuccotto is an Italian layered, bombe-type dessert. These cups, or coppas, have all of the delicious flavours of their larger cousin but are ready much more quickly.

2 tbsp flaked almonds
2 tbsp dark chocolate chips
juice and finely grated zest
   of 1 orange
1 tbsp brandy
300ml/10 1/2fl oz/scant 1 1/4 cups
   double cream
1/4 tsp vanilla extract
3 large chocolate muffins, cut into
   bite-sized cubes
1 tsp cocoa powder, to serve

1 Put the almonds in a dry frying pan and cook over a medium heat, stirring frequently, for 2–3 minutes, or until lightly browned and toasted. Immediately transfer them to a plate and set aside to cool. Meanwhile, put the chocolate chips in a small food processor and pulse until finely chopped.

2 Mix the orange juice and brandy together in a small bowl and set aside. Put the cream, vanilla extract and orange zest in a large bowl and whip, using an electric mixer, until soft peaks form.

3 Put half of the muffin cubes in four tall glasses or deep bowls and sprinkle with half of the almonds. Drizzle with half of the orange juice mixture and spoon half of the whipped cream over the top. Repeat the layers, then serve dusted with the cocoa powder.

hot fudge sundaes

Who can resist cold vanilla ice cream and hot chocolate fudge sauce? With this version, the sauce is ready so quickly, resistance truly is futile.

1 Remove the ice cream from the freezer and leave to stand at room temperature to soften slightly. Meanwhile, put the nuts in a dry frying pan and cook over a medium heat, stirring frequently, for 2–3 minutes until lightly browned and toasted. Immediately transfer them to a plate and set aside.

2 Meanwhile, make the sauce. Put the chocolate chips, cream, brown sugar, vanilla extract and butter in a saucepan and cook over a medium heat, stirring, for 1–2 minutes until the chocolate has just melted. Remove from the heat and stir until smooth.

3 Divide half of the ice cream into four sundae glasses or deep bowls, then spoon a little of the sauce over each. Add a second scoop of ice cream to each glass, spoon the remaining sauce over the top and sprinkle with the nuts. Serve immediately with wafers.

500ml/17fl oz/2 cups vanilla ice cream
4 tbsp chopped mixed nuts
wafers or crisp biscuits, such as cigarettes russes or fan wafers, to serve

HOT FUDGE SAUCE:
100g/3^1/$_2$oz/scant ^{1}/$_2$ cup dark chocolate chips
100ml/3^1/$_2$fl oz/scant ^{1}/$_2$ cup double cream
2 tbsp soft dark brown sugar
^{1}/$_2$ tsp vanilla extract
5g/^{1}/$_4$oz butter

panettone perdu

A sweet Italian fruit bread that is popular as a gift at Christmas, panettone provides the base for this delicious, comforting dessert.

1 Heat a 30cm/12in heavy-based frying pan over a medium heat. Meanwhile, put the eggs, milk, caster sugar and half of the vanilla extract together in a shallow dish and beat until well mixed. Put the cream, icing sugar and remaining vanilla extract in a bowl and whip, using an electric mixer, until soft peaks form, then set aside.

2 Melt the butter in the frying pan. Dip the panettone wedges into the egg mixture, turning them to coat thoroughly, then fry for 2 minutes on each side, or until golden brown.

3 Transfer the panettone to plates and dust with a little extra icing sugar. Serve hot with the berries and whipped cream.

4 eggs
4 tbsp milk
1 tsp caster sugar
^{1}/$_2$ tsp vanilla extract
125ml/4fl oz/^{1}/$_2$ cup double cream
1 tsp icing sugar, plus extra to serve
30g/1oz butter
4 thick wedges of panettone
85g/3oz/^{3}/$_4$ cup berries, such as blueberries or raspberries, to serve

knickerbocker glories (see age 76)

CHAPTER THREE

15-minute desserts

For creative confections that take just a quarter of an hour, it's time to turn on the heat. Grilling is great when you want to add a beautiful warm finish to billowing peaks of meringue, as in Lemon Meringue Pots, or give an Orange Soufflé Omelette a gloriously golden crust. Poaching fresh fruits lends a delicate, fully flavoured elegance to desserts such as Ginger-Poached Rhubarb with Real Custard. Deep-frying is another technique that can turn an after-dinner treat into something spectacular. Strawberry Samosas emerge in a flash from hot oil, their crisp, flaky pastry giving way to a soft, sweet, surprising filling. Or go all out and cool things off with festive Knickerbocker Glories for a classic ice cream sundae experience. Whatever you choose, these quick recipes are sure to win applause.

cheesey chimichangas with mango salsa

Chimichangas, filled and rolled tortillas, are popular street snacks in Mexico. This version is a sweet twist on the classic.

500ml/17fl oz/2 cups rapeseed oil, for deep-frying
200g/7oz/scant 1 cup cream cheese
1 tbsp icing sugar, plus extra for dusting
1/2 tsp vanilla extract
4 wheat tortillas or wraps

MANGO SALSA:
1 large mango, peeled, pitted and cut into small cubes
juice of 1 large lime
1 tsp icing sugar
1/2 mild red chilli, deseeded and finely chopped (optional)

1 To make the salsa, put the mango, lime juice, icing sugar and chilli, if using, in a bowl and toss well. Taste and add more sugar, if necessary, then set aside.
2 Heat the oil in a large heavy-based saucepan or deep-fat fryer over a medium heat until it reaches 180°C/350°F. Meanwhile, put the cream cheese, icing sugar and vanilla extract in a bowl and beat, using an electric mixer, for 1 minute until just combined. Put one-quarter of the cream cheese in the centre of 1 tortilla. Fold in the sides of the tortilla and then roll up from the bottom to enclose the filling. Secure the tortilla with a wooden cocktail stick, then repeat with the remaining filling and tortillas.
3 Working in batches, if necessary, to avoid overcrowding the pan, fry the chimichangas for 2-3 minutes, or until golden brown and crisp, turning once halfway through. Remove from the oil, using a slotted spoon, and drain on kitchen paper. Return the oil to the correct temperature before each batch.
4 Dust with icing sugar and serve hot with the mango salsa.

red berry mousses

This sweet, airy mousse makes a quick, delightful dessert.

450g/1lb/3²/₃ cups raspberries
4 tbsp redcurrant jelly or raspberry jam
1 egg white
250ml/9fl oz/1 cup double cream
2 tbsp icing sugar
4 mint sprigs, to decorate

1 Chill four freezerproof glasses or bowls in the freezer. Put the raspberries and jelly in a blender or food processor and blend for 1-2 minutes until puréed. Rub the purée through a fine sieve into a clean bowl to remove the seeds, then set aside.
2 Put the egg white in a clean bowl and whisk, using an electric mixer, until stiff peaks form, then set aside. Put the cream and icing sugar in another large bowl and whip for 2-3 minutes until soft peaks form (no need to wash the beaters first), then fold in the fruit purée. Fold in the egg white, using a large metal spoon.
3 Spoon the mousse into the chilled glasses and serve decorated with mint sprigs.

cherries jubilee

Originally invented to celebrate Queen Victoria's golden jubilee, this flambéed dessert has stood the test of time.

1 Put the cherries, caster sugar and 125ml/4fl oz/$^1/_2$ cup water in a medium frying pan. If you prefer not to flambé (see step 4), add the kirsch to the pan. Cook over a low heat, stirring occasionally, for 6–7 minutes until the sugar has dissolved and the cherries have thawed. Bring to the boil over a medium heat and boil for 5 minutes, or until the liquid has reduced by about half.

2 Meanwhile, mix together the arrowroot and 1 teaspoon cold water in a small bowl and set aside. Remove the ice cream from the freezer and leave to stand at room temperature to soften slightly.

3 Reduce the heat to low again and add the arrowroot mixture to the cherries. Cook, stirring continuously, for 1–2 minutes until the mixture has just thickened, then remove the pan from the heat.

4 To flambé the cherries, put the kirsch in a small saucepan over a medium heat until warm, then carefully ignite it with a match and pour it over the cherries, pouring away from you. Allow the alcohol to burn off and the flame to extinguish itself. Serve immediately with the ice cream.

225g/8oz/2 cups frozen pitted cherries
4 tbsp caster sugar
4 tbsp kirsch liqueur
$^1/_2$ tsp arrowroot
500ml/17fl oz/2 cups vanilla ice cream

blueberry & lemon brûlées

It's very hard to resist these delicious, individual brûlées.

1 Preheat the grill to high and fill a small roasting tin with iced water. Spoon the blueberries into four 200ml/7fl oz/scant 1-cup ramekins. Put the yogurt, lemon curd and lemon juice in a large bowl and mix until smooth. Put the cream in another bowl and whip, using an electric mixer, until soft peaks form, then fold it into the yogurt. Spoon the cream mixture over the blueberries and sprinkle with the caster sugar.

2 Put the ramekins in the tin of iced water; the water should reach three-quarters of the way up the sides of the ramekins. Grill, as close as possible to the heat source, for 1–2 minutes until the sugar melts. Remove from the heat and set aside for 1–2 minutes to allow the sugar to set a little before serving.

200g/7oz/1$^1/_3$ cups blueberries
4 tbsp Greek yogurt
2 tbsp lemon curd
1 tbsp lemon juice
250ml/9fl oz/1 cup double cream
4 tbsp caster sugar

▶ coconut snowballs

You don't need to wait for a blizzard to make these delightful, edible snowballs. For perfect ice cream balls, dip the scoop in hot water first.

500ml/17fl oz/2 cups coconut or vanilla ice cream
40g/1^1/$_2$oz/^{1}/$_2$ cup unsweetened desiccated coconut
1 tbsp icing sugar
2 tbsp chocolate chips
2 tbsp coconut flakes, preferably toasted

1 Line a baking sheet that will fit in your freezer with baking parchment. Divide the ice cream into 8 scoops on the parchment, then put the baking sheet in the freezer.

2 Set aside 1 tablespoon of the desiccated coconut and put the rest in a dry frying pan. Cook over a high heat, stirring occasionally, for 1–2 minutes until golden. Transfer to a plate, stir in the icing sugar and reserved desiccated coconut and set aside.

3 Put the chocolate chips in a heatproof bowl and rest it over a pan of gently simmering water, making sure the bottom of the bowl does not touch the water. Heat, stirring occasionally, for 2–3 minutes until the chocolate melts, then set aside.

4 Remove the baking sheet from the freezer and put the ice cream balls on a plate. Sprinkle with the coconut mixture and drizzle with the chocolate. Sprinkle with the coconut flakes and serve immediately.

15

15-minute desserts

nectarines with honey zabaglione

This honey-flavoured version of zabaglione, an Italian light custard made with Marsala wine, is perfect with summer stone fruits, such as nectarines.

4 nectarines or peaches, halved, pitted and thinly sliced
4 egg yolks
4 tbsp caster sugar
2 tbsp clear honey
4 tbsp Marsala wine
crisp biscuits, such as amaretti, to serve

1 Divide the nectarine slices into four large glasses or bowls and set aside. Put the egg yolks, caster sugar and honey in a heatproof bowl and rest it over a pan of simmering water, making sure the bottom of the bowl does not touch the water. Whisk, using an electric mixer, for 1–2 minutes until pale and frothy. Add the Marsala wine and whisk continuously for a further 6–8 minutes until the zabaglione is thick and pale and has trippled in volume.

2 Spoon the zabaglione over the nectarines and serve immediately with crisp biscuits.

strawberry samosas

Samosas are normally savoury, so filling them with juicy strawberries makes a lovely, sweet change.

1 Put 1 sheet of filo pastry on a work surface and keep the rest covered with a clean, damp tea towel while you work. Fold the filo sheet in half lengthways and then in half again and position it vertically in front of you. Put one-quarter of the strawberries at the bottom end of the pastry, leaving a little space between the edges of the pastry and the filling. Fold the bottom-right corner of the pastry diagonally up over the filling to form a triangle, then fold the lower left-hand corner up the left edge, keeping the triangular shape. Continue folding to the end to enclose the filling. Seal with oil, if needed, then repeat with the remaining pastry and filling. Keep the samosas covered with the damp tea towel.

2 Heat the oil in a large heavy-based saucepan or a deep-fat fryer until it reaches 180°C/350°F. Working in batches, if necessary, to avoid overcrowding the pan, fry the samosas for 2 minutes, or until golden brown and crisp, turning once halfway through. Remove from the oil, using a slotted spoon, and drain on kitchen paper. Dust with icing sugar while hot.

3 Warm the dulce de leche in a saucepan over a medium heat until runny, then drizzle it over the samosas. Serve warm with ice cream.

4 sheets of filo pastry, thawed if frozen
115g/4oz strawberries, hulled and cut into small cubes
500ml/17fl oz/2 cups rapeseed oil, for deep-frying and sealing
4 tbsp dulce de leche or caramel sauce
icing sugar, for dusting
250ml/9fl oz/1 cup vanilla ice cream, slightly softened, to serve

watermelon gazpacho

This is a wonderfully refreshing, fruity twist on the classic soup.

1 Put four freezerproof soup bowls in the freezer to chill. Working in batches, put the watermelon, strawberries, lime juice and caster sugar in a blender or food processor and blend for 1–2 minutes until puréed. Transfer to a large bowl, mix well and add more caster sugar to taste, if necessary. Rub the purée through a sieve into a clean bowl to remove any seeds. Thinly slice the reserved strawberries.

2 Pour the soup into the chilled bowls. Decorate with the sliced strawberries and mint sprigs and serve with meringues.

600g/1lb 5oz peeled and chopped seedless watermelon, well chilled
450g/1lb strawberries, hulled and halved, with 4 whole strawberries reserved for decoration
juice of 1 large or 2 small limes
4 tbsp caster sugar, plus extra to taste
4 mint sprigs, to decorate
ready-made meringues, to serve

indian mango with ginger & honey yogurt

Mango is a tender fruit that poaches very quickly. This recipe works really well with slightly underripe mangoes.

2 large, slightly underripe mangoes
4 tbsp caster sugar
6 cardamom pods

GINGER & HONEY YOGURT:
150g/5^{1}/$_{2}$oz/^{2}/$_{3}$ cup natural yogurt
^{1}/$_{2}$ tsp grated root ginger
1 tsp clear honey, or to taste

1 Peel the mangoes and cut the flesh away from the stones in long slices, then set aside.

2 Put the caster sugar, cardamom and 125ml/4fl oz/^{1}/$_{2}$ cup water in a saucepan and cook over a medium heat, stirring occasionally, for 1–2 minutes until the sugar has dissolved. Bring the syrup to the boil over a high heat and add the mango slices. Immediately reduce the heat as low as possible and poach for 3–5 minutes until tender.

3 Transfer the mango slices to four plates or bowls, using a slotted spoon. Increase the heat to high and return the syrup to the boil. Boil for 2–3 minutes or until reduced by half. Remove from the heat and set aside to cool slightly.

4 Meanwhile, put the yogurt in a bowl and stir in the ginger and honey, adding more honey to taste, if desired. Spoon the syrup over the mango slices and serve with the yogurt.

fruit cups

The sauce for this fruit salad is similar to a punch-type cocktail and reminiscent of long summer afternoons.

4 tbsp red vermouth
4 tbsp orange juice
2 tbsp gin
1 tbsp granulated sugar
2 large oranges
225g/8oz strawberries, hulled and halved or quartered, if large
^{1}/$_{4}$ honeydew or other green melon, peeled, deseeded and cut into bite-sized chunks
225g/8oz/heaped 2 cups raspberries
4 tbsp lemonade or ginger ale
4 mint sprigs, to decorate

1 Fill a sink with 10cm/4in iced water. Put the vermouth, orange juice, gin and granulated sugar in a saucepan over a medium heat and cook, stirring, for 1–2 minutes or until the sugar has dissolved. Bring to the boil over a high heat and boil for 1–2 minutes until the alcohol evaporates, then remove the pan from the heat, put it in the iced water and leave to cool, stirring occasionally.

2 Meanwhile, cut the peel and pith from the oranges, using a small serrated knife. Cut the orange into segments and put them in a large bowl. Add the strawberries, melon and raspberries.

3 Stir the lemonade into the syrup, then pour it over the fruit. Mix gently, then spoon the mixture into four tall glasses or deep bowls. Serve decorated with mint sprigs.

15-minute desserts

thai tropical fruit salad
with sweet chilli syrup

Dressed with sweet chilli syrup, this fruit salad has a little kick.

1 To make the syrup, put the sweet chilli sauce, icing sugar
  and 1 tablespoon water in a large bowl and stir until the sugar
  has dissolved, then set aside.

2 Cut the pineapple into bite-sized chunks, cutting on a lipped plate
  to catch and reserve the juice that is released. Add the pineapple
  and juice to the syrup, then add the mango and papaya. Peel
  the lychees, then peel the flesh away from the stones, adding
  the flesh to the bowl as you peel. Toss the fruit in the syrup.

3 Transfer the salad to four glasses or bowls. Serve decorated
  with mint leaves and with lime wedges for squeezing over.

1/4 large pineapple, peeled
  and cored
1 large mango, peeled, pitted
  and cut into bite-sized chunks
1 large papaya, peeled, deseeded
  and cut into bite-sized chunks
8 lychees
mint leaves, to decorate
1 lime, cut into wedges, to serve

SWEET CHILLI SYRUP:
1 tbsp bottled sweet chilli sauce
1 tbsp icing sugar

star fruit with ginger-thyme syrup

Star fruit look beautiful when sliced, and they make a stunning yet simple fruit salad that's just delicious.

2 large star fruit, thinly sliced

GINGER-THYME SYRUP:
100g/3¹/₂oz/scant ¹/₂ cup caster sugar
6 large thyme sprigs, plus extra thyme leaves for decoration
4cm/1¹/₂in piece root ginger, peeled and thinly sliced

1 To make the syrup, put the caster sugar, thyme sprigs, ginger and 100ml/3¹/₂fl oz/scant ¹/₂ cup water in a small saucepan and cook over a medium heat, stirring frequently, for 2 minutes until the sugar has dissolved. Bring to the boil over a high heat and boil for 2 minutes until slightly syrupy. Remove from the heat, stir in the star fruit and set aside to infuse for 5 minutes.

2 Remove the star fruit from the syrup, using a slotted spoon, and arrange on four plates or in bowls. Strain the syrup through a fine sieve over the star fruit and serve decorated with extra thyme leaves.

pineapple strudel

A strudel can be quick to make using filo pastry and a fruit such as pineapple that doesn't need lengthy cooking.

30g/1oz butter, melted
¹/₂ pineapple, peeled, cored and cut into 1cm/¹/₂in cubes
2 tbsp caster sugar
4 sheets of filo pastry, thawed if frozen
1 tsp icing sugar, to serve
whipped cream, to serve

1 Preheat the oven to 220°C/450°F/Gas 7 and brush a baking sheet generously with some of the melted butter. Put the pineapple and caster sugar in a bowl and toss together.

2 Put 1 sheet of filo pastry on a work surface and keep the rest covered with a clean, damp tea towel while you work. Generously brush the top of the filo sheet with butter, then layer another sheet on top of it, brush with butter and repeat with the remaining filo. Spoon the pineapple along one of the long edges of the pastry, leaving a 1cm/¹/₂in border at either end of the pastry. Roll up the filo from the filled edge, tucking in the short edges as you roll to enclose the pineapple.

3 Carefully transfer the strudel to the baking sheet and brush with butter. Bake for 10 minutes, or until golden brown and crisp. Carefully slide the strudel on to a serving plate, dust with the icing sugar and serve hot with whipped cream.

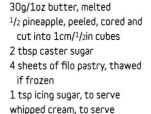

lemon meringue pots

Lemon meringue pie can take some time to make, but this crustless version is ready in minutes.

400ml/14fl oz tinned condensed
  milk
2 eggs, separated
juice and finely grated zest
  of 2 lemons
4 tbsp caster sugar

1 Put the condensed milk, egg yolks, and lemon juice and zest in a bowl and mix well. Divide the mixture into four 200ml/7fl oz/ scant 1-cup ramekins and freeze for 5 minutes.

2 Meanwhile, preheat the grill to high. Put the egg whites in a clean bowl and whisk, using an electric mixer, until stiff peaks form. Whisk in the caster sugar in a thin stream and continue whisking for 1–2 minutes, or until stiff and glossy.

3 Transfer the ramekins to a baking sheet and spoon the meringue over them. Make peaks in the meringue, using the tip of a knife. Grill for 2–3 minutes, or until the meringue has browned, watching carefully as it can burn easily. Serve immediately.

rum-buttered pineapple

Pineapple combined with rum is a great combination when you want to transport yourself mentally to the sunny Caribbean.

1 Remove the ice cream from the freezer and leave to stand at room temperature to soften slightly. Melt the butter in a 30cm/ 12in heavy-based frying pan over a medium heat. When it is foaming, add the pineapple. Cook for 4 minutes on each side until softened. Add the rum and cook for 2 minutes until the alcohol evaporates. Put the pineapple on four plates and set aside.

2 Reduce the heat to low and add the brown sugar and vanilla extract to the pan. Cook, stirring, for 1 minute, or until the sugar has dissolved. Spoon the sauce over the pineapple and serve immediately with the ice cream.

250ml/9fl oz/1 cup vanilla ice cream
30g/1oz butter
1 pineapple, peeled, cored and cut into 8 long slices
2 tbsp dark rum
2 tbsp soft dark brown sugar
1/4 tsp vanilla extract

orange soufflé omelette

An airy, puffed soufflé omelette is a lot quicker and easier to prepare than a classic soufflé – and it's almost as light. This one is prefect for sharing at the end of a romantic dinner for two.

1 Preheat the grill to high. Put the egg whites in a clean bowl and whisk, using an electric mixer, until medium peaks form. Put the yolks in a separate bowl, grate in the orange zest and add the marmalade and liqueur, if using. Whisk together using the mixer (no need to wash the beaters in between).

2 Heat a dry 20cm/8in non-stick frying pan with a flameproof handle over a medium heat. Fold the whisked whites into the yolk mixture, using a large metal spoon. Melt the butter in the frying pan, then gently spoon in the egg mixture, being careful not to knock out too much air. Cook the omelette for 3-4 minutes until golden underneath and starting to set.

3 Meanwhile, cut the peel and pith away from the orange, using a small serrated knife, then cut the flesh into segments and put them in a bowl. Put the frying pan under the grill and grill for 1-2 minutes until set and the top has browned. Gently fold the omelette in half and turn it out on to a large plate (or, cut it in half and serve on two plates, if preferred). Serve with the orange segments and cream.

SERVES 2
4 eggs, separated
1 orange
2 tbsp medium- or thick-cut orange marmalade
1 tbsp orange-flavoured liqueur, such as Cointreau (optional)
15g/1/2oz butter
single cream, to serve

▶ ginger-poached rhubarb with real custard

For this classic dessert, the rhubarb poaches quickly when cut into bite-sized pieces.

200g/7oz/scant 1 cup caster sugar, plus 2 tbsp extra
4cm/1¹/₂in piece root ginger, peeled and thinly sliced
450g/1lb rhubarb, cut into bite-sized pieces

REAL CUSTARD:
1 egg yolk
1 tbsp cornflour
2 tbsp caster sugar
200ml/7fl oz/scant 1 cup milk
200ml/7fl oz/scant 1 cup double cream

1 Put the caster sugar, ginger and 400ml/14fl oz/1²/₃ cups water in a large saucepan and cook over a medium heat, stirring occasionally, for 2–3 minutes until the sugar has dissolved. Bring to the boil over a high heat, then reduce the heat to as low as possible and add the rhubarb. Cook for 10–12 minutes until tender. Do not boil or the rhubarb will break up.

2 Meanwhile, make the custard. Put the egg yolk, cornflour, 2 tablespoons caster sugar and 4 tablespoons of the milk in a heatproof bowl. Put the remaining milk and the cream in a heavy-based saucepan and heat over a medium heat for 4 minutes until just boiling. Slowly pour the hot milk mixture into the egg yolk mixture in a thin stream, whisking continuously, then return the mixture to the pan and cook over a low heat, whisking continuously, for 5–6 minutes until thickened.

3 Spoon the hot rhubarb into four bowls and serve with the hot custard for pouring over.

cinnamon-caramel apples

Apples bathed in a slightly spicy caramel sauce make a simple yet delightfully indulgent dessert.

15g/¹/₂oz butter
100g/3¹/₂oz/scant ¹/₂ cup caster sugar
2 large green apples, such as Granny Smith, peeled, cored and each cut into 8 wedges
4 tbsp double cream
¹/₄ tsp cinnamon, plus extra to serve
Greek yogurt or crème fraîche, to serve

1 Melt the butter in a large non-stick frying pan over a medium heat. When it is foaming, add the caster sugar and 2 tablespoons water and cook, stirring, for 1–2 minutes until the sugar has dissolved. Add the apples and cook for 3–4 minutes, turning them over a couple of times, until they soften slightly.

2 Bring the mixture to the boil over a high heat and boil for 3–4 minutes, turning the apples frequently, until the sugar has turned a light caramel colour.

3 Remove from the heat and stir in the cream and cinnamon. Transfer the apples to four plates or bowls and spoon the sauce over them. Cool slightly, then dust with a little extra cinnamon and serve with yogurt alongside.

knickerbocker glories

The stripes in these sundaes resemble old-fashioned trousers, which inspired the name. They are always popular with children.

500ml/17fl oz/2 cups vanilla
  ice cream
4 tbsp dark chocolate chips
2 tsp golden syrup
15g/^{1}/$_2$oz butter
450g/1lb strawberries, hulled
2 tbsp icing sugar
squeeze of lemon juice
125ml/4fl oz/^{1}/$_2$ cup double cream
2 large peaches, halved and pitted,
  each half cut into 6 slices
225g/8oz/heaped 1^2/$_3$ cups
  raspberries
2 tbsp toasted flaked almonds,
  to decorate
4 maraschino cherries, drained,
  to decorate

1 Remove the ice cream from the freezer and leave to stand at room temperature to soften slightly. Put the chocolate chips, golden syrup and butter in a small saucepan and cook over a low heat, stirring frequently, for 3–4 minutes until the chocolate has just melted. Remove from the heat and set aside to cool slightly.

2 Meanwhile, put the strawberries, icing sugar and lemon juice in a blender or food processor and blend until puréed. Rub the purée through a fine sieve into a clean bowl to remove the seeds. Put the cream in a bowl and whip, using an electric mixer, until soft peaks form.

3 Put half of the peach slices in four sundae glasses or deep bowls. Add half of the raspberries and spoon half of the strawberry sauce over them. Add a scoop of ice cream to each glass, then repeat the layers again. Top each sundae with whipped cream, then drizzle with the chocolate sauce. Decorate with the almonds and maraschino cherries and serve.

fruit tostidas

Baked flour tortillas or wraps make a quick, unusual base for these fantastic fruit tarts.

4 small flour tortillas or wraps
15g/^{1}/$_2$oz butter, melted
85g/3oz/^{1}/$_2$ cup white chocolate
  chips
2 tbsp double cream
250g/9oz/1 cup ricotta cheese,
  drained
1 tbsp icing sugar
1 tsp vanilla extract
450g/1lb/2 cups strawberries,
  hulled and quartered

1 Preheat the oven to 200°C/400°F/Gas 6. Brush the tortillas with the melted butter and put them on two baking sheets. Bake for 8–9 minutes until golden brown and crisp. Meanwhile, put the chocolate chips and cream in a large heatproof bowl and rest it over a pan of gently simmering water, making sure the bottom of the bowl does not touch the water. Heat, stirring occasionally, for 2–3 minutes until the chocolate melts. Remove from the heat and set aside to cool slightly.

2 Put the ricotta, icing sugar and vanilla extract in a bowl and beat, using an electric mixer, for 1 minute until combined. Put the baked tortillas on four plates and spread the ricotta mixture over them. Sprinkle with the strawberries, drizzle with the chocolate sauce and serve.

palmiers with irish cream shots

These delicious layered biscuits are divine with rich Irish cream.

2/3 sheet of ready-rolled puff
   pastry, about 175g/6oz
1 tbsp clear honey
1 tbsp caster sugar
4 tbsp Irish cream whiskey,
   such as Baileys
2 tbsp coffee liqueur, such as
   Kahlúa
125ml/4fl oz/1/2 cup double cream
4 tbsp milk

1 Preheat the oven to 200°C/400°F/Gas 6 and line two baking
   sheets with baking parchment. Trim the pastry into a rectangle
   about 25 x 7.5cm/10 x 3in. Spread the honey thinly over the
   surface of the pastry, then sprinkle the caster sugar over it.
2 Fold the long edges of the pastry inwards so that they meet
   at the centre, then fold them in again. Finally, fold one long edge
   over the other, as if closing a book. Use a sharp knife to cut the
   pastry into 1cm/1/2in-thick slices to make about 20 palmiers.
3 Put the palmiers, cut-side up, on the baking sheets and bake for
   5 minutes. Turn the palmiers over, rotate the baking sheets and
   bake for a further 3–4 minutes until golden brown. Meanwhile,
   put the Irish cream, coffee liqueur, cream and milk in a small
   saucepan and warm over a medium heat, then pour into
   shot glasses. Serve the warm palmiers with the cream shots.

firecrackers

Firecrackers get their name from their shape, but they are also very snappy to make.

1 Put all of the ingredients for the dip in a bowl and stir until the sugar has dissolved, then set aside.

2 Put the dates and coconut in a bowl and stir in the orange juice $1/2$ teaspoon at a time until the mixture just holds together.

3 Heat the oil in a large heavy-based saucepan or deep-fat fryer over a high heat until it reaches 180°C/350°F and preheat the oven to 70°C/150°F/Gas $1/4$. Put 1 wonton wrapper on a clean work surface and dampen the edges with water. Put 1 teaspoon of the date mixture in the bottom left-hand corner, then roll the wrapper up diagonally from the filled corner. Pinch and slightly twist the ends of the roll to seal and make a Christmas cracker shape. Repeat with the remaining wonton wrappers and filling.

4 Working in batches to avoid overcrowding the pan, fry the firecrackers for 2 minutes, turning once, until golden brown. Remove from the oil, using a slotted spoon and drain on kitchen paper. Dust with the icing sugar and serve with the dip.

4 large pitted dates, finely chopped
5 tbsp unsweetened desiccated coconut
2 tsp orange juice
500ml/17fl oz/2 cups rapeseed oil, for deep-frying
16 wonton wrappers, thawed if frozen
1 tsp icing sugar, to serve

CHILLI-LIME DIP:
1 tbsp lime juice
1 tbsp bottled sweet chilli sauce
1 tbsp mirin
2 tsp caster sugar

classic crêpes

Thin, crisp pancakes with lemon and sugar always seem like a special treat, but they are quick and easy to make.

1 Preheat the oven to 70°C/150°F/Gas $1/4$ and heat a 30cm/12in heavy-based frying pan over a medium heat. Put the flour, egg, milk and salt in a blender and blend for 1–2 minutes until well mixed, then transfer to a jug.

2 Grease the frying pan with a little oil , then add enough of the crêpe mixture to thinly cover the base of the frying pan, tilting it as you pour to get an even coating. Fry the crêpe for 1 minute on each side until golden brown. Transfer to the oven to keep warm while you make the remaining 3 crêpes, greasing the pan with a little more oil between each one. Sprinkle with caster sugar and serve warm with lemon wedges for squeezing over.

100g/3$1/2$oz/heaped $3/4$ cup plain flour
1 egg
225ml/8fl oz/scant 1 cup milk
a pinch of salt
sunflower oil, for frying
caster sugar, to serve
lemon wedges, to serve

▶ salted peanut praline parfaits

You'll be amazed by how quickly you can whip up the praline in this recipe. Salted peanuts complement the caramel beautifully.

75g/2¹/₂oz/scant ²/₃ cup salted peanuts
150g/5oz/²/₃ cup caster sugar
sunflower oil, for greasing
125ml/4fl oz/¹/₂ cup double cream
500ml/17fl oz/2 cups vanilla ice cream, slightly softened
500ml/17fl oz/2 cups caramel ice cream, slightly softened

1 Line a baking sheet with baking parchment, spread the peanuts out in a single layer in the centre and set aside. Put the caster sugar and 3 tablespoons water in a small saucepan over a medium heat and cook for 2 minutes, stirring occasionally, until the sugar has dissolved. Bring to the boil over a high heat and boil for 3–4 minutes until it turns a caramel colour. Immediately pour the caramel over the peanuts and spread it out slightly, using a lightly greased palette knife. Leave to cool for 2 minutes, then carefully transfer the parchment to a cooling rack and leave to set in a cool place for 7–8 minutes. Meanwhile, put the cream in a bowl and whip, using an electric mixer, until soft peaks form, then set aside.

2 Break the praline into large pieces and reserve 4 for decoration. Put the rest in a plastic bag and crush to large crumbs with a rolling pin. Divide the vanilla ice cream into four glasses and sprinkle with half of the crushed praline. Add the caramel ice cream, then the remaining crushed praline. Top with the whipped cream and serve immediately with the reserved praline.

pecan-maple moneybags

The drawstring-purse shape of these wontons gives them the 'moneybag' name. This is an easy way to make bite-sized 'pies'.

15g/¹/₂oz butter, melted, plus extra for greasing
115g/4oz/1 cup pecan halves, chopped
4 tbsp maple syrup, plus extra to serve
12 wonton wrappers, thawed if frozen
250ml/9fl oz/1 cup vanilla ice cream, slightly softened, to serve

1 Preheat the oven to 200°C/400°F/Gas 6 and generously grease a baking sheet with melted butter. Put the pecans and maple syrup in a small bowl and mix well.

2 Put 1 wonton wrapper on a clean work surface and brush the edges with water. Put 1 teaspoon of the pecan mixture in the centre. To make a drawstring-purse shape, bring the corners of the wonton wrapper together and pinch just above the filling to seal. Repeat with the remaining wrappers and filling.

3 Put the moneybags on the baking sheet and brush generously with melted butter. Bake for 6–8 minutes until crisp and golden. Serve hot with ice cream and extra maple syrup drizzled over.

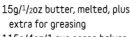

thai coconut pancakes

This street-food favourite from Thailand is so easy to make that it will surely become one of your favourites, too.

2 tbsp sunflower oil, for frying
115g/4oz/²/₃ cup rice flour or 115g/4oz/scant 1 cup plain flour
4 tbsp caster sugar
2 eggs
4 tbsp sweetened coconut cream, plus extra to serve
30g/1oz/¼ cup raisins
4 tbsp desiccated or fresh grated coconut

1 Heat 1¹/₂ teaspoons of the oil in a 20cm/8in non-stick frying pan over a medium heat and preheat the oven to 70°C/150°F/Gas ¹/₄. Put the flour, caster sugar, eggs and 125ml/4¹/₂fl oz/¹/₂ cup water in a blender and blend for 1–2 minutes until the batter is smooth and has the consistency of single cream. When the oil is hot, pour in one-quarter of the batter, tilting the pan to cover the base evenly.

2 Cook for 1–2 minutes until golden underneath and set on top. Spread 1 tablespoon of the coconut cream over the pancake and sprinkle with 1 tablespoon each of the raisins and coconut. Fold the pancake in half, turn it out on to a plate and keep warm in the oven. Repeat with the remaining batter and fillings to make 3 more pancakes, adding more oil to the pan before each one. Serve warm with extra coconut cream.

fruity french toast

Crisp brioche, fruity berry jam and fresh cream mean that this twist on French toast is destined to be a hit dessert.

4 tbsp raspberry jam
8 thin slices slightly stale brioche, challah or white bread
4 eggs
4 tbsp double cream, plus extra to serve
1 tbsp caster sugar
¹/₄ tsp vanilla extract
30g/1oz butter, for frying
icing sugar, to serve

1 Spread the jam over 4 slices of the bread and cover with the remaining slices of bread. Trim off and discard the crusts, if desired, then set the sandwiches aside. Put the eggs, cream, caster sugar and vanilla extract in a shallow dish and mix well.

2 Heat a 30cm/12in heavy-based frying pan over a medium heat. Put half of the butter in the pan and, while it melts, dip 2 of the sandwiches in the egg mixture, turning to coat on both sides. Add the sandwiches to the pan and fry for 2 minutes on each side until golden. Transfer to a plate and cover to keep warm while you make the remaining sandwiches.

3 Cut each sandwich in half and serve dusted with icing sugar and with extra cream.

brandy snap baskets

Thin, crisp brandy snaps are easily moulded into baskets, which you can serve with a variety of delicious fillings.

1 Preheat the oven to 190°C/375°F/Gas 5 and line two baking sheets with baking parchment. Fill a sink with 10cm/4in iced water and grease the outsides of four upturned 200ml/7fl oz/ scant 1-cup pudding basins or ramekins with oil. Put the caster sugar, butter and syrup in a small saucepan and cook over a low heat, stirring occasionally, for 3–4 minutes until all of the ingredients have melted and are blended.

2 Remove the pan from the heat and put it in the iced water for 1–2 minutes, stirring the mixture continuously, until cool, then remove from the water. Stir in the flour, lemon juice and ginger.

3 Drop 2 rounded teaspoonfuls of the brandy snap mixture on to each baking sheet, spacing well apart. Bake for 5–6 minutes until golden, then remove from the oven and leave to cool slightly, for about 30 seconds. Using a palette knife, lift the brandy snaps on to the greased basins and gently mould them around the basins, using your hands. Leave to cool for 1–2 minutes, then lift off and put the baskets right-side up on four plates. Fill with ice cream, top with berries and serve dusted with icing sugar.

sunflower oil, for greasing
2 tbsp caster sugar
30g/1oz butter
1 tbsp golden syrup
30g/1oz/¼ cup plain flour
squeeze of lemon juice
a large pinch of ground ginger
ice cream or whipped cream,
  to serve
mixed berries, to serve
icing sugar, to serve

white chocolate & lime mousses (see age 96)

CHAPTER FOUR

20-minute desserts

With twenty minutes, you have time to turn on the oven and create some stunning yet briskly made baked desserts. Puff pastry prefers a high heat, so you can bake it quickly, then split and fill it to make a simple but special Summer Cream Slice. Mocha Baked Alaskas need only a brief blast in the oven to brown the marshmallowy meringue coating and warm the chocolate cake base – the coffee ice cream centre stays firm to make a cool contrast. For a real show, fry up a spectacular batch of Mini Doughnuts with Jam. No one will guess that these warm, sugared sweethearts are made from a speedy scone-type dough. For chilled desserts, whip up White Chocolate & Lime Mousses or Mango & Ginger Trifle. Whatever you choose, these desserts will make the meal one to remember.

ricotta turnovers

If you've got a little extra time, serve these with the Grape Compôte on page 47, instead of the jam sauce.

125g/4^1/$_2$oz/^{1}/$_2$ cup ricotta cheese
2 tbsp ground almonds
4 tsp chopped mixed peel
2 tbsp caster sugar
^{1}/$_2$ tsp vanilla extract
2 sheets of ready-rolled puff
  pastry, about 425g/15oz in total
1 egg, beaten
4 tbsp apricot jam
1 tsp icing sugar

1 Preheat the oven to 200°C/400°F/Gas 6 and line two baking sheets with baking parchment. In a medium bowl, mix together the ricotta, almonds, mixed peel, caster sugar and vanilla extract and set aside.

2 Cut the pastry into 4 squares, each about 14cm/5^1/$_2$in square, put them on a chopping board and brush the edges with some of the egg. Divide the ricotta mixture on to the squares, positioning it slightly off-centre, towards the top right-hand corner. Fold the pastry over diagonally to make a triangle and enclose the ricotta. Seal the edges by pressing down with the tines of a fork, then transfer them to the baking sheet and brush with the remaining egg. Bake for 12–15 minutes until golden.

3 Meanwhile, put the jam and 1 tablespoon water in a small saucepan and warm over a low heat. Serve the turnovers dusted with the icing sugar and with the warm jam sauce.

crispy wonton mille-feuilles

Wonton wrappers, more conventionally used in Chinese cooking, become very crisp when baked – and ideal for layered desserts.

30g/1oz butter, melted
12 square wonton wrappers,
  thawed if frozen
1 tbsp icing sugar, plus extra
  to serve
125ml/4fl oz/^{1}/$_2$ cup double cream
^{1}/$_2$ tsp vanilla extract
125ml/4fl oz/^{1}/$_2$ cup Greek yogurt
100g/3^1/$_2$oz/^{2}/$_3$ cup blueberries
8 strawberries, hulled and
  quartered

1 Preheat the oven to 200°C/400°F/Gas 6 and generously grease two baking sheets with some of the melted butter. Brush both sides of each wonton wrapper with the butter, then dust one side with the icing sugar and transfer them to the baking sheets, sugared-sides up. Bake for 5 minutes until crisp, watching carefully as the corners can burn easily.

2 Transfer the wrappers to a wire rack and leave to cool for 5 minutes. Meanwhile, put the cream and vanilla extract in a large bowl and whip, using an electric mixer, until soft peaks form, then fold in the yogurt.

3 Put 1 wrapper on each of four plates and top with a heaped tablespoon of the cream mixture and some of the berries. Repeat the layering once more and top with the remaining wrappers, sugared-sides up. Dust with extra icing sugar and serve.

tea-poached prunes

Ready-to-eat dried fruit cooks much more quickly than traditional dried fruit, so keep some in your storecupboard. Prunes go well with the slightly citrus notes of Earl Grey tea.

1 Put the prunes, tea bags, caster sugar, lemon zest and 600ml/ 21fl oz/scant 2½ cups boiling water in a large saucepan and bring to the boil over a high heat. Boil for 5 minutes until the sugar has dissolved.
2 Reduce the heat to low, remove the tea bags and simmer, covered, for 12 minutes, or until the prunes are plump and tender. Remove from the heat and remove and discard the lemon zest.
3 Spoon the prunes into four heatproof glasses or bowls with a little of the syrup. Serve with crème fraîche for spooning over.

350g/12oz/heaped 1½ cups pitted ready-to eat dried prunes
2 Earl Grey tea bags
140g/5oz/⅔ cup caster sugar
2.5 cm/1in pared strip of lemon zest
crème fraîche, to serve

peaches & pecans with quick sablés

Sablés are crisp biscuits made from sweetened pastry. They go perfectly with the mellow flavours of peaches and maple syrup.

1 Preheat the oven to 200°C/400°F/Gas 6 and line a baking sheet with baking parchment. To make the sablés, cut out 8 rounds from the pastry, using a 2.5cm/1in biscuit cutter. Brush the rounds with the egg and sprinkle the caster sugar over them in a thin layer. Transfer to the baking sheet and bake for 10–12 minutes until golden brown and slightly caramelized on top. Transfer to a wire rack and set aside to cool.
2 Meanwhile, melt the butter in a large frying pan over a medium heat. When it foams and is slightly brown, add the peaches and cook for 3–5 minutes, turning once, until beginning to soften. Add the pecans and maple syrup and bring to the boil over a high heat. Boil for 1 minute, then remove from the heat and gently stir in the cream. Spoon the peaches into four bowls and serve warm with the sablés.

30g/1oz butter
4 peaches, halved, pitted and each half halved again
2 tbsp chopped pecans
4 tbsp maple syrup
2 tbsp double cream

QUICK SABLÉS:
225g/8oz ready-rolled shortcrust pastry
1 egg, beaten
2 tbsp caster sugar

mango & ginger trifles

Sweet mango and spicy ginger make fabulous partners here.

1 Put the grated ginger, icing sugar and 2 tablespoons water in a small bowl and stir until the sugar has dissolved. Put the mango flesh in another bowl and stir in half of the ginger mixture and 4 teaspoons of the preserved ginger.

2 Put the orange juice and ginger wine, if using, in a shallow bowl and mix well. Put the biscuits in four glasses or bowls and drizzle over the orange juice mixture, pushing the biscuits down into the liquid. Add the mango mixture and set aside.

3 Put the cream in a bowl and whip, using an electric mixer, until soft peaks form, then fold in the remaining grated ginger mixture and spoon it over the mango. Sprinkle with the remaining preserved ginger and serve decorated with mint leaves.

2.5cm/1in piece root ginger, peeled and finely grated
4 tbsp icing sugar
1 large mango, peeled, pitted and cut into bite-sized pieces
2 tbsp chopped preserved or crystallized ginger
125ml/4fl oz/$^1/_2$ cup orange juice
2 tbsp ginger wine, such as Stone's, or sweet sherry (optional)
8 sponge finger biscuits, broken into pieces
250ml/9fl oz/1 cup double cream
mint leaves, to decorate

buttermilk scones with quick raspberry 'jam'

When matched with a warm jam-like mixture and billowing clouds of cream, scones makes a luxurious dessert.

1 Preheat the oven to 200°C/400°F/Gas 6 and lightly dust a baking sheet with flour. Mix the flour and salt together in a large bowl. Rub in the butter until the mixture resembles breadcrumbs, then stir in three-quarters of the buttermilk and all but 2 tablespoons of the granulated sugar. Mix to make a slightly soft dough, adding more buttermilk, if necessary.

2 Turn the dough out on to a lightly floured surface and roll it out to 2cm/$^3/_4$in thick. Cut out 8 scones, using a 4cm/1$^1/_2$in round biscuit cutter. Re-roll the trimmings as necessary. Brush the tops with the remaining buttermilk and bake for 12–14 minutes until risen and golden brown.

3 Meanwhile, heat the raspberries and the reserved granulated sugar in a saucepan over a medium heat, stirring occasionally, for 2–3 minutes until the sugar has dissolved. Bring to a boil over high heat and boil, stirring occasionally, for 8 to 10 minutes until thick. Serve the scones with the warm 'jam' and whipped cream.

225g/8oz/2 cups self-raising flour, plus extra for dusting and rolling
225g/8oz/heaped 1 cup caster sugar
200g/7oz/scant 1$^2/_3$ cups raspberries
$^1/_4$ tsp salt
55g/2oz cold butter, diced
150ml/5fl oz/scant $^2/_3$ cup buttermilk or 125ml/4fl oz/ $^1/_2$ cup natural yogurt
whipped cream, to serve

►fruit shortcake tart

A sweet scone mixture can be used to make a quick tart base, which is perfect for topping with summer fruit.

175g/6oz/heaped 1¹/₃ cups
self-raising flour, plus extra
for rolling
¹/₄ tsp salt
40g/1¹/₂oz cold butter, diced
2 tbsp caster sugar
6 tbsp milk
225g/8oz/scant 1 cup mascarpone
cheese
1 tsp icing sugar, plus extra
to serve
finely grated zest of ¹/₂ lemon
1 peach or nectarine, halved,
pitted and sliced
225g/8oz/1¹/₂ cups strawberries,
hulled and halved
100g/3¹/₂oz/scant 1 cup
raspberries
clear honey, for drizzling

1 Preheat the oven to 200°C/400°F/Gas 6. Put the flour and salt in a large bowl and stir well, then rub in the butter until the mixture resembles breadcrumbs. Stir in the caster sugar and 5 tablespoons of the milk and stir to make a soft dough, adding the remaining milk, if necessary.

2 Transfer the dough to a sheet of baking parchment on a work surface and use a lightly floured rolling pin to roll it out into a 20cm/8in round. Lift the parchment and dough on to a baking sheet and bake for 12–14 minutes until risen and golden brown.

3 Meanwhile, put the mascarpone, icing sugar and lemon zest in a bowl and beat, using an electric mixer, for 1–2 minutes until smooth. Carefully transfer the baked tart base to a serving plate, using a fish slice or palette knife. Spread the mascarpone mixture over the base and arrange the fruit on top. Serve drizzled with honey and dusted with icing sugar.

gingered seared pears

A blast in a hot pan and a good dose of warming ginger are quick ways to pep up simple pears.

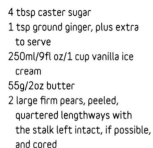

4 tbsp caster sugar
1 tsp ground ginger, plus extra
to serve
250ml/9fl oz/1 cup vanilla ice
cream
55g/2oz butter
2 large firm pears, peeled,
quartered lengthways with
the stalk left intact, if possible,
and cored

1 Heat a dry large heavy-based frying pan over a medium heat. Mix the caster sugar and ginger together on a large plate. Remove the ice cream from the freezer and leave to stand at room temperature to soften slightly.

2 Melt the butter in the pan. When it foams and is slightly brown, roll the pear quarters in the sugar mixture to coat on all sides. Cook for 3 minutes on each side, including the curved side, spooning the pan juices over them, until tender and slightly glazed.

3 Transfer the pears to plates and spoon the pan juices over them. Dust with a little extra ginger and serve hot with the ice cream.

lemon-polenta cupcakes

Polenta, or cornmeal, gives cakes a fine, crumbly texture and yellow colour. These cupcakes make a lovely gluten-free dessert.

115g/4oz butter, softened
115g/4oz/$^1/_2$ cup caster sugar
115g/4oz/heaped 1 cup ground almonds
55g/2oz/$^1/_3$ cup quick-cook polenta
$^1/_2$ tsp gluten-free baking powder
1 tsp vanilla extract
1 egg, plus 1 egg yolk
a large pinch of salt
juice and finely grated zest of 1 lemon
4 tbsp icing sugar
crème fraîche, to serve

1 Preheat the oven to 200°C/400°F/Gas 6 and line a muffin tin with 8 paper cupcake cases. Put the butter, caster sugar, almonds, polenta, baking powder, vanilla extract, egg, egg yolk and salt in a food processor and blend for 1 minute until combined. Add the lemon zest and 1 tablespoon of the lemon juice and pulse 2 or 3 times to mix. Spoon the mixture evenly into the cupcake cases and bake for 12-14 minutes until the tops are browned and firm. Rotate the tin halfway through baking.

2 While the cupcakes are baking, mix the icing sugar with 1 tablespoon of the remaining lemon juice to make a syrup.

3 Carefully lift the warm cupcakes from the muffin tin, using a palette knife, and peel off the paper cases. Transfer the cupcakes to bowls, spoon over the syrup and serve with crème fraîche.

barbados creams

This taste of the Caribbean, with bananas, rum and dark brown sugar, makes a festive quick dessert.

1 tbsp white rum
1 tbsp lime juice
1 tbsp caster sugar
4 bananas, peeled and sliced
250ml/9fl oz/1 cup double cream
1 tsp vanilla extract
1 tsp icing sugar
4 tbsp Greek yogurt
4 tbsp soft dark brown sugar

1 Put the rum, lime juice and caster sugar in a large bowl and stir until the sugar has dissolved. Add the bananas and toss them gently in the mixture to prevent discolouration, then leave to stand for 5 minutes to soften.

2 Meanwhile, put the cream, vanilla extract and icing sugar in a bowl and whip, using an electric mixer, until soft peaks form. Fold in the yogurt and set aside. Put the brown sugar and 1 tablespoon water in a small saucepan and cook over a medium heat, stirring occasionally, for 2 minutes until the sugar has dissolved and the mixture is just bubbling. Remove from the heat.

3 Spoon the bananas into four glasses or bowls and spoon any juices left in the bowl over them. Top with the cream and drizzle the brown sugar sauce over the top. Serve immediately.

summer cream slice

This quicker version of the classic mille-feuille is bursting with the sweet, sunshine-packed flavours of summer.

1 Preheat the oven to 200°C/400°F/Gas 6 and line two baking sheets with baking parchment. Cut 4 rectangles from the pastry, each about 11 x 7.5cm/4^1/$_4$ x 3in, and put them on the baking sheets. Prick all over with a fork and gently brush the tops with the egg. Bake for 12–15 minutes until risen, golden and crisp.

2 Meanwhile, put the cream, vanilla extract and 1 teaspoon of the icing sugar in a bowl and whip, using an electric mixer, until soft peaks form, then set aside.

3 Transfer the pastries to a chopping board, using a fish slice or palette knife, and use a small, serrated knife to split the pastry in half horizontally, then leave to cool slightly.

4 Put each pastry base on a plate, top with some of the whipped cream and arrange the fruit on top. Cover with the top halves of the pastry, dust with the remaining powdered sugar and serve.

1 sheet of ready-rolled puff pastry, about 250g/9oz
1 egg, beaten
185ml/6fl oz/^{3}/$_4$ cup double cream
1 tsp vanilla extract
2 tsp icing sugar, plus extra to serve
225g/8oz/1^1/$_2$ cups strawberries, hulled and thinly sliced
1 peach, halved, pitted and thinly sliced
85g/3oz/^{1}/$_2$ cup raspberries

cherry jalousies

The classic 'shutter' puff-pastry pie is made here in miniature version, with juicy tinned cherries.

1 Preheat the oven to 220°C/450°F/Gas 7 and line two baking sheets with baking parchment. Lightly flour a work surface and roll out the pastry to about half of its original thickness. Cut out 8 rectangles, each about 10 x 8cm/4 x 3in.

2 Put 4 pieces of pastry on the baking sheets, brush the edges with some of the egg and arrange 6 cherries on top of each rectangle. Make 3 or 4 vertical cuts in the centre of each remaining piece of pastry, leaving the border of each piece intact, and position these over the cherries. Press the edges of the top and bottom pastries together to seal and brush the tops with the egg. Bake for 15 minutes, or until risen, golden and crisp.

3 Meanwhile, put the reserved cherry syrup in a saucepan and bring to the boil over a high heat. Boil for 5–6 minutes until thick enough to coat the back of a spoon. Remove from the heat and stir in any remaining cherries. Serve the jalousies hot with whipped cream and the cherry syrup spooned alongside.

plain flour, for rolling
2 sheets of ready-rolled puff pastry, about 375g/13oz in total
1 egg, beaten
400g/1lb tinned cherries in syrup, drained and syrup reserved
whipped cream, to serve

plums in port

If you want to create a fabulous dessert but the fruit you have on hand isn't quite ripe, poaching is the ideal technique to use. A sweet, spice-infused port syrup goes beautifully with plums.

1 Put the port, caster sugar, star anise and 250ml/9fl oz/1 cup water in a saucepan and cook over a medium heat, stirring occasionally, for 2–3 minutes until the sugar has dissolved. Bring to the boil over a high heat and boil for 3 minutes, then reduce the heat to very low.

2 Add the plums and leave to simmer, covered, for 12–15 minutes, turning halfway through, until tender.

3 Remove the star anise and transfer the plums into bowls. Drizzle with some of the cooking liquid and serve with crème fraîche and a little nutmeg grated over them.

250ml/9fl oz/1 cup ruby port
225g/8oz/heaped 1 cup caster sugar
2 star anise
8 large plums, halved, pitted and each half halved again
crème fraîche or Greek yogurt, to serve
freshly grated nutmeg, to serve

white chocolate & lime mousses

Fresh citrus and sweet chocolate meld into a delicious dessert.

100g/3½oz/scant ⅔ cup white chocolate chips
250ml/9fl oz/1 cup double cream
finely grated zest of 2 large or 4 small limes
juice of 1 large or 2 small limes
2 tbsp icing sugar

1 Put four 200ml/7fl oz/scant 1-cup ramekins or freezerproof glasses in the freezer to chill. Put the chocolate chips and 2 tablespoons of the cream in a heatproof bowl and rest it over a pan of gently simmering water, making sure the bottom of the bowl does not touch the water. Heat, stirring occasionally, for 2–3 minutes until the chocolate has melted. Remove from the heat and set aside to cool slightly.

2 Meanwhile, put the remaining cream in a bowl and whip, using an electric mixer, until soft peaks form. Add one-quarter of it to the melted chocolate and whisk until smooth, then fold the chocolate mixture and half of the lime zest back into the whipped cream.

3 Spoon the mixture into the ramekins and freeze for 8–10 minutes until slightly firmed. Meanwhile, put the lime juice and icing sugar in a small bowl and stir until the sugar has dissolved. Remove the mousses from the freezer, sprinkle with the remaining zest and spoon the lime syrup over them. Serve immediately.

apricot puff bites

These mini pastries, inspired by the Danish classic, use just a few simple ingredients that are easy to keep to hand.

plain flour, for rolling
1 sheet of ready-rolled puff pastry, about 250g/9oz
1 egg, beaten
4 tbsp apricot jam
2 tbsp icing sugar

1 Preheat the oven to 200°C/400°F/Gas 6 and line two baking sheets with baking parchment. On a lightly floured surface, using a lightly floured rolling pin, roll out the pastry to about half its original thickness. Cut out 12 rectangles, each about 10 x 8cm/ 4 x 3in, then brush the edges with the egg.

2 Put 1 tablespoon of the jam on one half of each rectangle. Fold the other half over to cover the filling and press the edges together to seal. Transfer to the baking sheets and bake for 10 minutes, or until risen, golden and crisp. Meanwhile, mix together the icing sugar and ½ teaspoon water to make a thick but pourable icing. Add more water, if necessary.

3 Serve the puff bites warm, drizzled with the icing.

bananas with pecan praline

Crunchy caramel-coated pecans give this dessert extra appeal.

4 tbsp caster sugar
55g/2oz/½ cup pecan halves
500ml/17fl oz/2 cups caramel or
   maple ice cream
100g/3½oz/scant ⅔ cup dark
   or milk chocolate chips
4 tbsp double cream
4 bananas

1 Line a baking sheet that will fit in your freezer with baking parchment and put it in the freezer. Put the caster sugar and 3 tablespoons water in a non-stick frying pan and cook over a medium heat, stirring occasionally, for 1–2 minutes until the sugar has dissolved. Bring to the boil over a high heat and boil for 4–5 minutes until the sugar turns a medium caramel colour.

2 Add the pecans and boil for a further 1 minute, then pour the pecans out on to the cold baking sheet, spreading them out as much as possible. Leave to cool for 1 minute, then lift the parchment on to a wire rack and leave to cool for 4–5 minutes until set and brittle. Remove the ice cream from the freezer and leave to stand at room temperature to soften slightly.

3 Meanwhile, put the chocolate chips and cream in a small saucepan and cook over a very low heat, stirring occasionally, for 3–4 minutes until the chocolate has melted. Peel and slice the bananas and arrange them on four plates. Sprinkle the pecans over the top, breaking up any that have stuck together, and top with the ice cream. Drizzle with the chocolate sauce and serve.

raspberry cranachan

Grilling the oats and sugar, rather than toasting them in the oven, makes this version of the Scottish speciality much quicker.

1 Preheat the grill to high and line a grill pan with foil. Mix the oats and sugar together and spread the mixture out on the foil. Grill for 4-5 minutes, stirring frequently, until the sugar has melted and the oats are lightly toasted. Watch carefully, as the sugar can burn easily. Remove from the grill and leave to cool for 5 minutes.

2 Meanwhile, put the cream in a large bowl and whip, using an electric mixer, until soft peaks form, then fold in the whisky and honey. Stir the oat mixture and crumble up any large lumps.

3 Put half of the raspberries in four glasses or bowls and spoon half of the whipped cream over them. Sprinkle with half of the oat mixture, then layer again. Serve drizzled with extra honey and whisky and decorated with the almonds and extra raspberries.

75g/2^1/$_2$oz/^{3}/$_4$ cup rolled oats, preferably jumbo
3 tbsp soft light brown sugar
250ml/9fl oz/1 cup double cream
1 tbsp whisky, plus extra to serve
2 tbsp clear honey, plus extra to serve
225g/8oz/heaped 1^2/$_3$ cups raspberries, plus extra to decorate
1 tbsp toasted flaked almonds, to decorate

crêpes suzette

This quick version of the classic French dessert always impresses.

1 Preheat a 30cm/12in heavy-based frying pan over a medium heat. Meanwhile, put the flour, egg, milk and salt in a blender and blend for 1-2 minutes until well mixed, then transfer to a jug.

2 Grease the frying pan with oil and pour in enough of the crêpe batter to thinly cover the base of the pan, tilting the pan as you pour to coat it evenly. Cook the crêpe for 1 minute on each side, or until golden brown. Fold into quarters and transfer to a plate. Repeat while you make the remaining 3 crêpes, greasing the pan with a little more oil between each one.

3 Melt the butter in the pan. When it is foaming, stir in the marmalade and orange juice. Add the crêpes and cook for 1 minute, then remove from the heat. Put the liqueur in a small saucepan and warm it over a low heat, then carefully ignite it with a match and pour it over the crêpes, pouring away from you. Allow the alcohol to burn off and the flame to extinguish itself, then spoon the crêpes and sauce on to four plates and serve immediately with cream.

100g/3^1/$_2$oz/heaped ^{3}/$_4$ cup plain flour
1 egg
225ml/8fl oz/scant 1 cup milk
a pinch of salt
sunflower oil, for frying
15g/1^1/$_2$oz butter
4 tbsp orange marmalade
2 tbsp orange juice
4 tbsp orange-flavoured liqueur, such as Grand Marnier
single cream, to serve

►mini doughnuts with jam

Using self-raising flour instead of yeast in this dough cuts down on the time it takes to make these delicious doughnuts.

500ml/17fl oz/2 cups rapeseed oil,
  for deep-frying
4 tbsp raspberry jam
225g/8oz/1³/4 cups self-raising
  flour, plus extra
  for rolling
2 tsp baking powder
5 tbsp caster sugar
150ml/5fl oz/scant ²/3 cup milk

1 Heat the oil in a large heavy-based saucepan or deep-fat fryer over a high heat until it reaches 180°C/350°F. Put the jam and 2 tablespoons water in a small saucepan and bring to the boil over a high heat. Boil, stirring occasionally, for 1 minute until the jam melts. Transfer to small dipping bowls and set aside.

2 Meanwhile, put the flour, baking powder and 2 tablespoons of the caster sugar in a large bowl and mix well. Add three-quarters of the milk and stir to make a soft dough, adding more milk as needed. Turn out the dough on to a lightly floured work surface and roll it out to 1cm/¹/2in thick. Cut out rounds of dough, using a 4.5cm/1³/4in round biscuit cutter, then cut out the centre holes using a 2.5cm/1in cutter. Gather together and re-roll the trimmings, as necessary, to make 24 mini doughnuts.

3 Working in batches to avoid overcrowding the pan, fry the doughnuts for 2 minutes until puffed and golden, turning once halfway through. Remove from the oil, using a slotted spoon, and drain on kitchen paper. Return the oil to the correct temperature between batches. Toss the doughnuts in the remaining caster sugar and serve warm with the jam for dipping.

warm fig & honey salad

This honey-scented dessert is a great choice when you want to give a meal a sophisticated finale.

12 large ready-to-eat dried figs
4 tbsp clear honey
2 strips pared orange zest
Greek yogurt, to serve

1 Put the figs, honey, orange zest and 500ml/17fl oz/2 cups water in a saucepan large enough to hold the figs snugly in a single layer. Cook over a medium heat for 30 seconds, or until the honey has dissolved. Bring to the boil over a high heat, then reduce the heat to low and simmer, uncovered, for 15 minutes until the figs are tender. Remove the figs from the pan, using a slotted spoon, and arrange on four plates.

2 Remove and discard the orange zest from the liquid, then bring to the boil over a high heat and boil for 2–3 minutes until syrupy. Spoon the syrup over the figs and serve topped with yogurt.

lemon cheesecakes

Making mini cheesecakes in ramekins, rather than in a large cake tin, means they're ready to serve in minutes.

70g/2¹/₂oz gingernut biscuits
40g/1¹/₂oz butter
200g/7oz/scant 1 cup cream cheese
4 tbsp Greek yogurt
4 tbsp icing sugar
juice and finely grated zest of 1 large lemon
single cream, to serve (optional)

1 Put the biscuits in a small plastic bag and crush to fine crumbs, using a rolling pin, then set aside. Melt the butter in a small saucepan over a medium heat, then remove the pan from the heat, add the biscuit crumbs and stir until well coated in the butter. Press the crumbs firmly into the base of four 200ml/7oz/²/₃ cup ramekins and freeze for 5 minutes.

2 Meanwhile, put the cream cheese in a large bowl and beat, using an electric mixer, for 1–2 minutes until smooth, then beat in the yogurt, icing sugar, and lemon juice and zest until well mixed.

3 Spoon the cheesecake mixture into the ramekins, then freeze for a further 5 minutes. Serve with a little cream, if desired.

almond-amaretti bombes

These bombes are a creative way to end a meal.

500ml/17fl oz/2 cups vanilla ice cream
55g/2oz/¹/₂ cup flaked almonds
10 amaretti biscuits
1 tbsp amaretto liqueur, to serve

1 Remove the ice cream from the freezer and leave to stand at room temperature to soften slightly. Line a baking sheet that will fit in your freezer with baking parchment and put it in the freezer. Put the almonds in a dry frying pan and cook over a medium heat, stirring frequently, for 3–4 minutes, until golden. Set aside 1 tablespoon of the toasted almonds for decoration and transfer the rest to a food processor.

2 Crumble the biscuits into the food processor and blend for 1 minute or until the mixture resembles coarse crumbs. Spread the crumbs out on a large tray or baking sheet. Scoop half of the ice cream into 4 balls, put them on the tray and roll to coat in the crumbs. Use forks to help manoeuvre the ice cream balls.

3 Transfer the coated ice cream balls to the chilled baking sheet and return it to the freezer, then repeat with the remaining ice cream to make 4 more bombes. Add them to the chilled baking sheet and freeze for 5–10 minutes to firm up.

4 Divide into four bowls and serve decorated with the reserved almonds and splashed with a few drops of the amaretto.

chocolate freezer squares

Melted chocolate studded with fruits and nuts sets very quickly if popped in the freezer. This recipe uses a mix of milk and dark chocolate, but you can use all dark chocolate if you prefer.

1 Line a 20cm/8in square cake tin with baking parchment, leaving enough parchment to hang over the sides of the tin. Put the milk and dark chocolate chips, butter and golden syrup in a heavy-based saucepan and heat over a low heat for 3-4 minutes, stirring occasionally, until just melted. Do not allow the mixture to boil.

2 Remove the mixture from the heat and stir in the biscuits, pistachios and raisins. Pour the mixture into the tin and immediately put it in the freezer for 10 minutes until firm.

3 Lift the chocolate square out of the tin, using the overhanging baking parchment, then cut or break it into squares and serve. Store leftovers in the fridge.

SERVES 8

150g/5^{1}/$_{2}$oz/scant 1 cup milk chocolate chips
150g/5^{1}/$_{2}$oz/scant 1 cup dark chocolate chips
115g/4oz butter, cubed
2 tbsp golden syrup
4 shortbread finger biscuits, each broken into 8 pieces
4 tbsp chopped pistachios
30g/1oz/^{1}/$_{4}$ cup raisins

mocha baked alaskas

Coffee and chocolate make a great combination in this rich and indulgent version of a baked Alaska.

1 Preheat the oven to 220°C/425°F/Gas 7 and line a baking sheet with baking parchment. Remove the ice cream from the freezer and leave to stand at room temperature to soften slightly. Cut 1 round from each of the brownies, using a 7cm/2³/₄in round biscuit cutter and put them on the baking sheet. Sprinkle with the liqueur, if using.

2 Put the egg whites in a clean bowl and whisk, using an electric mixer, until stiff peaks form. Whisk in the caster sugar in a thin stream and continue whisking until stiff and glossy. Put 1 scoop of ice cream on each of the brownie circles.

3 Working quickly, spoon the meringue over the ice cream and use a palette knife to spread it all the way down the sides of the Alaskas, making sure the ice cream and brownies are completely covered. Make a few peaks in the meringue, using the tip of the knife. Bake for 6–7 minutes until the meringue is browned. Dust with a little cocoa powder and serve immediately.

250ml/9fl oz/1 cup coffee ice cream
4 large chocolate brownies
1 tbsp coffee liqueur, such as Kahlúa (optional)
4 egg whites
115g/4oz/1/2 cup caster sugar
cocoa powder, to decorate

monte bianco expresso

The espresso-strength coffee in these chestnut and chocolate treasures creates a dessert with kick.

1 Put the chocolate chips in a heatproof bowl and rest it over a pan of gently simmering water, making sure the bottom of the bowl does not touch the water. Heat, stirring occasionally, for 2–3 minutes until the chocolate has melted. Remove from the heat.

2 Meanwhile, put the cream, vanilla extract and icing sugar in a bowl and whip, using an electric mixer, until soft peaks form.

3 Put the coffee and 2 tablespoons boiling water in a large heatproof mixing bowl and stir until dissolved. Add the chestnut purée, caster sugar and melted chocolate and beat, using the electric mixer (no need to wash the beaters in between), until just combined.

4 Spread the chocolate-chestnut purée over the meringue nests, top with whipped cream and serve dusted with cocoa powder.

2 tbsp dark chocolate chips
125ml/4fl oz/1/2 cup double cream
1/2 tsp vanilla extract
1/2 tsp icing sugar
1 tsp instant coffee granules
140g/5oz/1/3 cup unsweetened chestnut purée
2 tbsp caster sugar
4 ready-made meringue nests
1 tsp cocoa powder, to decorate

baby banana muffins with maple whipped cream

These mini banana muffins with a cream topping are so delicious, they'll disappear in minutes.

1 small banana, peeled
2 tbsp soft light brown sugar
2 tbsp sunflower oil
1 egg yolk
55g/2oz/^{1}/$_2$ cup self-raising flour
^{1}/$_4$ tsp cinnamon
a pinch of salt
30g/1oz/^{1}/$_4$ cup chopped pecans
125ml/4fl oz/^{1}/$_2$ cup double cream
2 tbsp maple syrup, plus extra
   to serve

1 Preheat the oven to 180°C/350°F/Gas 4 and line a mini muffin tin with 12 mini paper cupcake cases. Put the banana in a food processor and pulse until chopped, then add the brown sugar, oil, egg yolk, flour, cinnamon and salt. Blend for 1–2 minutes until just combined. Add the pecans and pulse 2 or 3 times to mix, then spoon the mixture evenly into the paper cases.
2 Bake for 12 minutes until the muffins are risen and firm to the touch. Meanwhile, put the cream in a bowl and whip, using an electric mixer, until stiff peaks form, then fold in the maple syrup.
3 Serve the muffins with the whipped cream and drizzled with extra maple syrup.

ciocolatto in carozza

'In carozza' means 'in a carriage' in Italian and is the term for a French toast sandwich. This version has a very indulgent filling.

8 thin slices of white bread,
   preferably slightly stale
4 squares of dark or milk
   chocolate, about 15g/^{1}/$_2$oz each
4 eggs
1 tbsp caster sugar
^{1}/$_4$ tsp vanilla extract
30g/1oz butter
single cream, to serve

1 Put 4 slices of the bread on a chopping board and put 1 square of chocolate in the centre of each one. Cover with the remaining slices of bread and press down around the chocolate to seal well. Trim off the bread crusts, leaving a border of about 1.5cm/^{5}/$_8$in all around the chocolate. (Alternatively, cut out round sandwiches, using a 9cm/3^1/$_2$in biscuit cutter.)
2 Heat a large heavy-based frying pan over a medium heat. Beat the eggs, caster sugar and vanilla extract in a shallow bowl and dip 2 of the sandwiches in the egg, turning to coat both sides.
3 Melt half of the butter in the frying pan and, when it is foaming, add the egg-coated sandwiches and fry for 2 minutes on each side until golden. Transfer to two plates and cover with two upside-down plates to keep warm while you make the remaining 2 sandwiches. Drizzle with cream and serve warm.

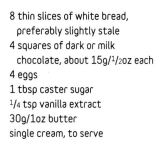

cinnamon twists with hot chocolate dip

This is a speedy take on Spanish churros. Although churros are usually eaten for breakfast, this flaky version makes a more-than-satisfying dessert.

1 Preheat the oven to 200°C/400°F/Gas 6 and line two baking sheets with baking parchment. Mix 1 tablespoon of the caster sugar with the cinnamon and set aside. Cut the puff pastry into 12 strips, each about 14cm/5$^{1}/_{2}$in long and 1.5cm/$^{5}/_{8}$in wide. Brush both sides of the strips with the egg and sprinkle with the cinnamon sugar. Put them on the baking sheets, twisting each one 3 or 4 times. Bake for 10 minutes until risen, golden and crisp.

2 Meanwhile, to make the dip, put the cream and chocolate chips in a small saucepan and cook over a low heat for 2 minutes, stirring continuously, until the chocolate has melted. Remove from the heat and stir in the vanilla extract, then pour the chocolate sauce into ramekins or small bowls.

3 Serve the cinnamon twists hot with the sauce for dipping.

4 tbsp caster sugar
$^{1}/_{4}$ tsp cinnamon
$^{3}/_{4}$ sheet of ready-rolled puff pastry, about 200g/7oz
1 egg, beaten

HOT CHOCOLATE DIP:
125ml/4fl oz/$^{1}/_{2}$ cup double cream
115g/4oz/$^{2}/_{3}$ cup dark chocolate chips
$^{1}/_{2}$ tsp vanilla extract

poires belle hélène (see page 121)

CHAPTER FIVE

25-minute desserts

In twenty-five minutes you can turn out fantastic desserts in double-quick time – whether you want to end your meal on a light, fruity note or cap it off with something more decadent. Scrumptious Lemon Sponge Puddings come together with hardly any effort at all when you simply blend together all of the ingredients for the cakes in a food processor. Minutes later, they're baking in the oven, and your hands are free to make the sweet-tart sauce that will provide the perfect finishing touch. From light-as-a-cloud Passionfruit Floating Islands and succulent Summer Berry Shortcakes to rich Black-Bottomed Lime Cheesecakes and airy Chocolate Soufflés, you'll find the options here truly tantalizing.

sticky coconut rice with mangoes

Kao Niow Ma Muang, as this is called in Thailand, is a popular family dessert.

200g/7oz/1 cup jasmine rice
200ml/7fl oz/scant 1 cup milk, plus extra as needed
400ml/14fl oz/1²/₃ cups coconut milk
4 tbsp caster sugar
2 small mangoes, peeled, pitted and cut into large slices

1 Put the rice, milk and half of the coconut milk in a saucepan and bring to the boil over a high heat, stirring. Reduce the heat to low, cover and leave to simmer for 20 minutes, or until the rice is tender. Add a splash of extra milk if the mixture gets too dry.

2 Meanwhile, put the remaining coconut milk and the caster sugar in a separate saucepan and bring to the boil over a medium heat, stirring until the sugar has dissolved. Cook for 10 minutes, stirring frequently, until reduced to about 4 tablespoons.

3 Stir the coconut milk mixture into the cooked rice, then spoon the rice into four bowls. Serve topped with the mango slices.

hot banana soufflés

Quick and impressive, these soufflés are also low in fat.

melted butter, for greasing
55g/2oz/¹/₄ cup caster sugar, plus 4 tsp for dusting
2 large bananas, peeled
1 egg yolk
1 tbsp lemon juice
3 egg whites
single cream, to serve

1 Preheat the oven to 200°C/400°F/Gas 6 with a baking sheet inside. Generously grease four 200ml/7fl oz/scant 1-cup ramekins with butter and dust the inside of each one with 1 teaspoon of the caster sugar. Put the bananas, egg yolk, lemon juice and 1 tablespoon of the caster sugar in a food processor and blend to a purée. Scrape the purée into a large bowl and set aside.

2 In a separate clean bowl, whisk the egg whites, using an electric mixer, until stiff peaks form. Whisk in the remaining caster sugar in a thin stream, whisking continuously until the meringue is stiff and glossy. Stir one-quarter of the meringue into the banana purée to lighten it, then fold in the rest.

3 Spoon the mixture into the ramekins, filling them to the brim. Level the tops with a palette knife, scraping off and discarding any excess soufflé mixture. Bake on the preheated baking sheet for 15 minutes until risen. Drizzle with cream and serve immediately.

fig tarts

For a quick and elegant dessert, try these delicious tarts.

1 Preheat the oven to 200°C/400°F/Gas 6 and line two baking
  sheets with baking parchment. Cut out 4 rounds from the pastry,
  using a sharp knife and an upturned 11cm/4^1/$_4$in-wide coffee cup
  or saucer as a guide. Transfer the rounds to the baking sheets
  and prick them all over with a fork.
2 Arrange 3 fig halves on each pastry round, cut-sides up, and
  brush the edges of the pastry with the egg. Bake for 15 minutes,
  or until the pastry is risen, golden and crisp and the figs have
  softened slightly.
3 Dust with icing sugar and carefully transfer to four plates. Serve
  hot with crème fraîche.

2 sheets of ready-rolled puff
  pastry, about 500g/1lb 2oz
6 large figs, halved lengthways
1 egg, beaten
icing sugar, to serve
crème fraîche, to serve

tropical baked alaskas

Tangy fresh pineapple is a great foil for sweet meringue in these
mini baked Alaskas.

1 Preheat the oven to 220°C/425°F/Gas 7 and line a baking sheet
  with baking parchment. Remove the sorbet from the freezer and
  leave to stand at room temperature to soften slightly.
2 Cut out 4 rounds of sponge cake, using a 7cm/2^3/$_4$in round biscuit
  cutter. Put the pineapple rings on the sponge rounds and trim
  around the edge of the pineapple so it is the same size as the
  cake base. Cut the trimmings into smaller pieces and pack them
  into the centre of the pineapple rings, where the core used to be
  (you may not need all of the trimmings). Transfer the cake and
  pineapple stacks to the baking sheet and set aside.
3 Put the egg whites in a clean bowl and whisk, using an electric
  mixer, until stiff peaks form. Whisk in the caster sugar in a thin
  stream, whisking continuously until stiff and glossy.
4 Put 1 scoop of the sorbet on each pineapple ring. Working quickly,
  spoon the meringue over the sorbet and use a palette knife to
  spread the meringue all the way down the sides, making sure the
  sorbet and cake are completely covered. Make a few peaks in the
  meringue, using the tip of the knife. Bake for 6–7 minutes, until
  browned. Transfer to four plates and serve immediately.

250ml/9fl oz/1 cup mango sorbet
  or ice cream
4 slices of loaf-type vanilla sponge
  cake
^{1}/$_2$ pineapple, peeled, cored and cut
  crossways into 4 thick rings
4 egg whites
115g/4oz/^{1}/$_2$ cup caster sugar

upside-down mango tart

Tropical fruits, such as mango, are a great choice for quick, upside-down tarts.

1 sheet of ready-rolled puff
   pastry, about 250g/9oz
30g/1oz butter, melted
1 tbsp caster sugar
1/2 tsp vanilla extract
1 large, slightly underripe mango,
   peeled, pitted and cut into
   2cm/3/4in slices
whipped cream, to serve

1 Preheat the oven to 200°C/400°F/Gas 6. Using a sharp knife and an upturned 20cm/8in pie dish as a guide, cut out a circle from the pastry, then set aside.

2 Sprinkle the butter, caster sugar and vanilla extract in the base of the pie dish and cover with the mango slices, packing them closely together and trimming, where necessary, to fit. Gently lay the pastry over the mango, tucking it in slightly around the edges.

3 Bake for 20 minutes, or until the pastry is golden brown and crisp. Lay a serving plate over the top of the pie dish and, using oven mitts or a folded dish towel to protect your hands, carefully invert the pie dish to turn the tart on to the serving plate, fruit-side up. Reposition any loose pieces of mango, using the tip of a knife, then slice the tart and serve with whipped cream.

berry hob cobbler

This cobbler topping is steamed, rather than baked, speeding up cooking time and resulting in sweet little dumplings.

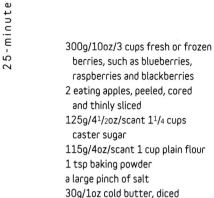

300g/10oz/3 cups fresh or frozen
   berries, such as blueberries,
   raspberries and blackberries
2 eating apples, peeled, cored
   and thinly sliced
125g/4 1/2oz/scant 1 1/4 cups
   caster sugar
115g/4oz/scant 1 cup plain flour
1 tsp baking powder
a large pinch of salt
30g/1oz cold butter, diced
6 tbsp milk
1/2 tsp vanilla extract
whipped cream, to serve

1 Put the berries, apples and 4 tablespoons water in a deep frying pan or wok with a lid. Set aside 2 tablespoons of the caster sugar and add the rest to the pan. Bring to the boil over a medium heat, then reduce the heat to low, cover and cook for 10 minutes until the juices have run from the berries and the apples have softened slightly.

2 Meanwhile, put the flour, baking powder and salt in a large bowl and mix. Rub in the butter until the mixture resembles breadcrumbs, then stir in the reserved caster sugar. Mix together the milk and vanilla extract, then stir it into the flour, 1 tablespoon at a time, to make a soft, slightly damp dough (you may not need all of the milk). Uncover the pan and drop teaspoonfuls of the dough on to the fruit. Simmer, covered, for 15 minutes, or until the dough has cooked through and the fruit has softened. Spoon into bowls and serve with whipped cream.

pink peaches with vanilla crème fraîche

For a light, pretty treat, try this fabulous summer dessert of peaches poached in a rosé-wine syrup.

750ml/26fl oz/3 cups rosé wine
300g/10^{1}/$_{2}$oz/1^{1}/$_{3}$ cups caster sugar
1 vanilla pod, split lengthways
4 peaches, halved and pitted
6 tbsp crème fraîche
1 tbsp icing sugar

1 Put the wine, caster sugar and half of the vanilla pod in a large saucepan and bring to the boil over a medium heat. Cook, stirring occasionally, for 2–3 minutes until the sugar has dissolved. Reduce the heat to low, add the peaches and leave to simmer for 15 minutes, turning over halfway through, until tender. Make sure the liquid doesn't boil.

2 Meanwhile, put the crème fraîche and icing sugar in a bowl. Using the tip of a sharp knife, scrape the seeds from the remaining half of the vanilla pod into the bowl and mix well.

3 Remove the peaches from the pan, using a slotted spoon, and set aside to cool slightly. Discard the vanilla pod and half of the poaching liquid, then bring the remaining liquid to the boil. Boil for 4–5 minutes until syrupy. Meanwhile, carefully peel the skins from the peaches and discard. Transfer the peaches to four heatproof bowls or glasses, spoon a little of the syrup over them and serve with the crème fraîche.

berry-ginger crumbles

Berries cook quickly, so they're perfect for fast desserts. The spicy ginger topping here complements them beautifully.

175g/6oz/heaped 1 cup fresh or frozen blueberries
175g/6oz/heaped 1^{1}/$_{3}$ cups fresh or frozen raspberries
4 tbsp caster sugar
115g/4oz/scant 1 cup plain flour
55g/2oz cold butter, diced
1 tsp ground ginger
a pinch of salt
4 tbsp demerara sugar
vanilla ice cream, to serve

1 Preheat the oven to 180°C/350°F/Gas 4. Pack the berries into four 200ml/7fl oz/scant 1-cup ramekins and evenly sprinkle with the caster sugar.

2 Put the flour, butter, ginger and salt in a food processor and blend until the mixture resembles breadcrumbs. Add the demerara sugar and pulse 3 or 4 times to combine, then spoon the topping over the berries.

3 Put the ramekins on a baking sheet and bake for 20 minutes, or until the filling is bubbling and the topping is golden brown and crunchy. Serve hot with ice cream.

black-bottomed lime cheesecakes

The lime and dark chocolate combination is slightly unusual but delicious. The chocolate in the cheesecake base helps the biscuit crumbs and butter to firm up very quickly.

75g/2¹/₂oz digestive biscuits
40g/1¹/₂oz butter
2 tbsp dark chocolate chips
115g/4oz/scant ¹/₂ cup cream cheese
finely grated zest of 2 limes
juice of 1¹/₂ limes
2 tbsp icing sugar
100ml/3¹/₂fl oz/scant ¹/₂ cup double cream

1 Put a baking sheet in the freezer to chill. Put the biscuits in a plastic bag and crush to fine crumbs, using a rolling pin. Melt the butter in a small saucepan over a medium heat, then remove from the heat, add the chocolate chips and stir until melted. Stir in the biscuit crumbs until well coated, then press the mixture firmly into the bases of four 9cm/3¹/₂in loose-bottomed tart tins.

2 Put the tart tins on the chilled baking sheet and freeze for 5 minutes. Meanwhile, put the cream cheese in a large bowl and beat, using an electric mixer, for 1–2 minutes until smooth. Reserve a generous pinch of the lime zest for decoration and add the rest to the cheese, along with the lime juice and icing sugar. Beat until just combined, then add the cream and beat for 1–2 minutes until smooth and thickened. Spoon the cheesecake mixture over the biscuit bases and freeze for 10 minutes.

3 Carefully loosen the bases from the tins and lift out. Dip a palette knife in hot water, wipe dry and use it to transfer the cheesecakes to four plates. Serve sprinkled with the reserved lime zest.

apple streusels

The streusel mixture in this version of a classic recipe does a time-saving double act, baking into both a shortbread-like base and a crumbly topping.

1 Preheat the oven to 200°C/400°F/Gas 6 with a baking sheet inside. Put the flour, caster sugar, almonds, butter and salt in a food processor and pulse 8–10 times until the mixture resembles large crumbs. Be careful not to overwork the mixture or it will form a dough.

2 Divide three-quarters of the streusel mixture into four 200ml/ 7fl oz/scant 1-cup ramekins and press firmly into the base. Sprinkle the raisins over the streusel mixture, then top with the apples, pressing down so the filling is below the rim of the ramekins. Sprinkle the remaining streusel mixture over the top.

3 Bake on the preheated baking sheet for 17–20 minutes, or until the topping is golden brown. Serve hot with cream.

115g/4oz/scant 1 cup plain flour
45g/1¹/₂oz/¹/₃ cup caster sugar
2 tbsp ground almonds
85g/3oz cold butter, diced
a pinch of salt
30g/1oz/¹/₄ cup raisins
2 eating apples, peeled and grated
single cream or vanilla ice cream,
    to serve

baked nectarines with almond crumbs

Amaretti biscuits make a lovely sweet and crunchy topping for ripe nectarines.

1 Preheat the oven to 180°C/350°F/Gas 4 and grease a baking dish large enough to hold the nectarine halves upright in a single layer with melted butter. Put the nectarines, cut-sides up, in the dish.

2 Put the biscuits in a small bag and crush to crumbs, using a rolling pin. Transfer to a small bowl and stir in the almonds, caster sugar and butter. Press 1 teaspoon of the crumb mixture into the indentation in each nectarine (where the stone used to be) and scatter any remaining crumbs over the top.

3 Bake for 18–20 minutes, or until the nectarines have softened and the topping has browned slightly. Transfer to four bowls and serve with whipped cream.

4 small nectarines, halved
    and pitted
8 amaretti biscuits
30g/1oz/¹/₃ cup ground almonds
3 tbsp caster sugar
30g/1oz butter, melted, plus extra
    for greasing
whipped cream, to serve

▸ passionfruit floating islands

The 'floating islands' in this French favourite are actually clouds of quickly poached meringue. The sharp passionfruit sauce contrasts with their marshmallow-like sweetness.

4 wrinkly, ripe passionfruit, halved
2 tbsp orange juice
1 tbsp icing sugar
300ml/10^{1}/$_{2}$fl oz/scant 1^{1}/$_{4}$ cups milk
2 egg whites
4 tbsp caster sugar

1 Scoop the passionfruit seeds and pulp into a bowl. Stir in the orange juice and icing sugar and set aside. Put the milk and 300ml/10^{1}/$_{2}$fl oz/scant 1^{1}/$_{4}$ cups water in a saucepan and bring to the boil over a medium heat, then reduce the heat to low, so that it is steaming hot but not bubbling.

2 Put the egg whites in a clean bowl and whisk, using an electric mixer, until stiff peaks form. Whisk in the caster sugar in a thin stream and continue whisking until the meringue is stiff and glossy. Take 1 heaped dessertspoon of meringue and use a second spoon to shape it into a quenelle, or egg shape, then drop it into the hot milk.

3 Working in batches to avoid overcrowding the pan, poach the meringues for 2 minutes on each side, then transfer to four plates, using a slotted spoon. Serve with the passionfruit sauce.

ricotta, apple & raisin hotcakes

Ricotta makes these surprisingly speedy hotcakes light and meltingly tender.

^{1}/$_{2}$ large eating apple, cored
115g/4oz/^{1}/$_{2}$ cup ricotta cheese
4 tbsp milk
2 eggs, separated
a pinch of salt
1 tbsp caster sugar
85g/3oz/^{3}/$_{4}$ cup self-raising flour
30g/1oz/^{1}/$_{4}$ cup raisins
sunflower oil, for frying
Greek yogurt or crème fraîche, to serve
clear honey, to serve

1 Heat a 30cm/12in heavy-based frying pan over a medium heat and preheat the oven to 70°C/150°F/Gas ^{1}/$_{4}$. Grate the apple into a large bowl and stir in the ricotta, milk, egg yolks, salt and sugar. Fold in the flour and raisins. Put the egg whites in a clean bowl and whisk, using an electric mixer, until stiff peaks form, then fold into the ricotta mixture, using a large metal spoon.

2 Grease the frying pan with a little oil. Working in batches, pour 3 tablespoons of the mixture into the pan to form 1 hotcake, adding as many hotcakes as will fit in the pan. Cook for 2 minutes until golden brown on the bottom, then flip over and cook for a further 2 minutes. Transfer the hotcakes to a plate and keep warm in the oven while you make the rest.

3 Serve topped with yogurt and drizzled with honey.

lime filo tart

Delicate filo pastry, tart lime and rich condensed milk team up here to form a delicious, alluring tart.

40g/1¹/₂oz butter, melted
4 sheets of filo pastry
400ml/14fl oz tinned condensed
  milk, ideally chilled
250ml/9fl oz/1 cup double cream
juice and finely grated zest
  of 3 large limes
1 tsp icing sugar, to serve
lime wedges (optional), to serve

1 Preheat the oven to 200°C/400°F/Gas 6 and generously grease two baking sheets with some of the melted butter. Put 1 sheet of filo pastry on a work surface and keep the rest covered with a clean, damp tea towel while you work. Brush the filo with butter, then fold in half, short end to short end. Brush with butter and fold again, this time long end to long end.

2 Cut the folded filo crossways into 3 rectangles and transfer to one of the baking sheets. Repeat with the remaining filo and butter to make a total of 12 rectangles. Bake for 5–7 minutes, rotating the baking sheets halfway through, if necessary, until brown and crisp. Transfer the baked filo rectangles to a wire rack and leave to cool slightly.

3 Meanwhile, put the condensed milk, cream and lime juice and zest in a large bowl that will fit in your freezer and beat, using an electric mixer, until thickened, then freeze for 10 minutes.

4 Put 1 filo rectangle on each of four plates. Spread half of the lime filling over the 4 rectangles, then layer again and top with a third filo rectangle. Serve dusted with icing sugar and with lime wedges, if desired, for squeezing over.

muhallabia

You can serve this Middle Eastern version of rice pudding hot for a quick dessert, but it is also popular chilled.

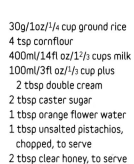

30g/1oz/¹/₄ cup ground rice
4 tsp cornflour
400ml/14fl oz/1²/₃ cups milk
100ml/3fl oz/¹/₃ cup plus
  2 tbsp double cream
2 tbsp caster sugar
1 tbsp orange flower water
1 tbsp unsalted pistachios,
  chopped, to serve
2 tbsp clear honey, to serve

1 Put the rice, cornflour and one-quarter of the milk in a large saucepan and stir until smooth, then whisk in the rest of the milk, along with the cream and caster sugar. Bring to the boil over a medium heat, stirring continuously, until the sugar has dissolved.

2 Reduce the heat to low and simmer, stirring frequently, for 20 minutes, or until thickened.

3 Remove from the heat and stir in the orange flower water. Spoon the pudding into four heatproof bowls and serve sprinkled with the pistachios and drizzled with the honey.

poires belle hélène

This classic French combination of poached pears with rich chocolate sauce is elegant and quick.

1 Put the caster sugar, lemon zest and 750ml /26fl oz/3 cups water in a saucepan and bring to the boil over a medium heat. Boil, stirring occasionally, for 2–3 minutes until the sugar has dissolved, then reduce the heat to low.

2 Meanwhile, peel the pears, leaving the stalks intact, and trim a small piece from the base of each of the pears so that they can stand upright on a plate. Put the pears in the saucepan and poach in the syrup over a low heat for 18–20 minutes, turning halfway through, until tender. Make sure the liquid doesn't boil.

3 While the pears are cooking, make the chocolate sauce. Put the chocolate chips, cream and vanilla extract in a small saucepan over a low heat and cook, stirring, for 2–3 minutes until smooth and the chocolate has melted. Using a slotted spoon, transfer the pears to four plates and serve with the hot sauce spooned over them.

250g/9oz/1 cup plus 2 tbsp caster sugar
thinly pared zest of $1/2$ lemon
4 ripe pears
200g/7oz/heaped 1 cup dark chocolate chips
185ml/6fl oz/$3/4$ cup double cream
$1/4$ tsp vanilla extract

►lemon sponge puddings

These individual lemon sponges are coated in a satiny smooth lemon sauce.

115g/4oz butter, softened, plus extra for greasing
140g/5oz/⅔ cup caster sugar
2 eggs plus 1 yolk
115g/4oz/¾ cup plus 2 tbsp self-raising flour
juice and finely grated zest of 1 large lemon, plus extra zest to decorate
a pinch of salt
2 tsp cornflour
crème fraîche, to serve

1 Preheat the oven to 180°C/350°F/Gas 4 and grease four 200ml/7fl oz/scant 1-cup ramekins. Set aside 2 tablespoons of the caster sugar and put the rest in a food processor. Add the butter, whole eggs, flour, lemon zest and salt and blend for 1–2 minutes until just combined. Spoon the mixture into the moulds and bake for 18–20 minutes until risen, brown and firm to the touch.

2 Meanwhile, make the sauce. Put the egg yolk, cornflour and lemon juice in a bowl and whisk well. Put the reserved caster sugar and 100ml/3½fl oz/ scant ½ cup water in a saucepan and heat over a medium heat, stirring, for 30 seconds or until the sugar has dissolved. Pour it on to the egg mixture in a thin stream, whisking continuously. Return the mixture to the pan and cook over a low heat, whisking continuously, for 2 minutes or until thickened.

3 Turn out the cakes and put them right-side up on four plates. Spoon the sauce over them and serve warm with crème fraîche and extra lemon zest to decorate.

summer tiramisù

Raspberry and orange give this speedy dessert a bright flavour.

2 eggs, separated
4 tbsp caster sugar
225g/8oz/scant 1 cup mascarpone cheese
4 tbsp orange juice
2 tbsp orange-flavoured liqueur, such as Cointreau
12 sponge finger biscuits, each broken into 2–3 pieces
100g/3½oz/scant 1 cup raspberries, plus extra to decorate
55g/2oz white chocolate, chopped
1 tsp icing sugar
4 mint sprigs, to decorate

1 Put the egg whites in a clean bowl and whisk, using an electric mixer, until soft peaks form. Put the egg yolks, caster sugar and mascarpone in another bowl and beat with the mixer (no need to clean the beaters first) until just smooth. Stir in a little of the whisked egg whites to lighten, then fold in the rest.

2 Stir the orange juice and liqueur together in a shallow bowl. Dip half of the biscuit pieces into the liquid and put them in four large glasses or bowls. Sprinkle half of the raspberries over the top, then follow with half of the mascarpone mixture. Dip the remaining biscuits and layer again with the raspberries and mascarpone, then sprinkle the chopped chocolate over the top.

3 Dust with the icing sugar and serve decorated with extra raspberries and mint sprigs.

cherry clafoutis

The classic French dessert bakes quickly if you make it in individual ramekins.

1 Preheat the oven to 200°C/400°F/Gas 6 with a baking sheet inside and grease four 200ml/7fl oz/scant 1-cup ramekins with oil. Divide the cherries into the ramekins.

2 Put the flour, caster sugar, eggs and milk in a blender and blend for 1–2 minutes until well mixed and smooth, then carefully pour the mixture into the ramekins and press 1 fresh cherry, if using, into the top of each one. Bake on the preheated baking sheet for 20 minutes, or until puffed and brown.

3 Dust the clafoutis with the icing sugar, drizzle with cream, if desired, and serve hot.

sunflower oil, for greasing
175g/6oz/1^1/$_2$ cups fresh or
   frozen pitted cherries, plus
   4 fresh cherries with stems for
   decoration (optional)
40g/1^1/$_2$oz/^{1}/$_3$ cup plain flour
2 tbsp caster sugar
2 eggs
125ml/4fl oz/^{1}/$_2$ cup milk
1 tsp icing sugar, to serve
single cream (optional), to serve

summer berry shortcakes

Shortcakes are rich scones that are a popular American summer dessert when paired with ripe, juicy berries.

1 Preheat the oven to 200°C/400°F/Gas 6 and grease a baking sheet with butter. Mix together the flour, baking powder and salt in a large bowl. Rub in the butter until the mixture resembles breadcrumbs, then stir in the caster sugar.

2 Put the egg and 4 tablespoons of the cream in a bowl and whisk well. Mix 4 tablespoons of the egg mixture into the flour, 1 tablespoon at a time, to make a soft, slightly damp dough, adding more liquid, if needed. Turn out the dough on to a lightly floured surface and roll it out to 1cm/^{1}/$_2$in thick. Cut out 4 shortcakes, using a 7cm/2^3/$_4$in round biscuit cutter, then gather up and reroll the trimmings and cut out 4 more shortcakes.

3 Transfer the shortcakes to the baking sheet and brush the tops with any remaining egg mixture. Bake for 15 minutes, or until risen and golden brown. Meanwhile, toss the strawberries, mixed berries and icing sugar together in a small bowl. In another bowl, whip the remaining cream, using an electric mixer, until soft peaks form. Serve the warm shortcakes halved and sandwiched with the cream and berries.

115g/4oz cold butter, diced, plus
   extra for greasing
225g/8oz/scant 2 cups plain flour,
   plus extra for rolling
2 tsp baking powder
^{1}/$_4$ tsp salt
2 tbsp caster sugar
1 egg
250ml/9fl oz/1 cup double cream
4 large strawberries, hulled
   and quartered
150g/5^1/$_2$oz/1 cup mixed
   berries, such as blueberries
   and raspberries
1 tbsp icing sugar

warm loaded oatmeal cookies

These cookies are packed with chocolate, nuts and raisins – flavours you won't be able to resist.

55g/2oz butter, softened
85g/3oz/¹/₃ cup caster sugar
1 egg yolk
1 tsp vanilla extract
75g/2¹/₂oz/³/₄ cup rolled oats
55g/2oz/¹/₃ cup plus 2 tbsp
  plain flour
¹/₄ tsp bicarbonate soda
a pinch of salt
30g/1oz/¹/₄ cup raisins
30g/1oz/¹/₄ cup chopped pecan
  nuts or walnuts
2 tbsp milk chocolate chips
ice cream, to serve

1 Preheat the oven to 180°C/350°F/Gas 4 and line two baking sheets with baking parchment. Put the butter, caster sugar, egg yolk, vanilla extract, oats, flour, bicarbonate of soda and salt in a large bowl and beat, using an electric mixer, until just combined. Stir in the raisins, nuts and chocolate chips.

2 Divide the mixture into 12 equal portions, roll them into balls and put them on the baking sheets, then flatten to about 1cm/¹/₂in thick. Bake for 12–15 minutes until golden brown around the edges. Remove the ice cream from the freezer and leave to stand at room temperature to soften slightly.

3 Slide the baking parchment and cookies on to wire racks and leave to cool for 2–3 minutes. Carefully transfer the cookies to four plates, using a spatula to move them because they will be soft. Serve warm with ice cream.

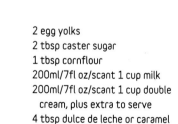

caramel brioche puddings

A luxurious variation on everyday bread and butter pudding.

2 egg yolks
2 tbsp caster sugar
1 tbsp cornflour
200ml/7fl oz/scant 1 cup milk
200ml/7fl oz/scant 1 cup double
  cream, plus extra to serve
4 tbsp dulce de leche or caramel
  sauce, plus extra to serve
2 thick slices of brioche, torn into
  bite-sized pieces

1 Preheat the oven to 180°C/350°F/Gas 4. Whisk together the egg yolks, caster sugar, cornflour and 2 tablespoons of the milk in a large heatproof bowl and set aside.

2 Put the cream, dulce de leche and the remaining milk in a saucepan and bring to the boil over a high heat, stirring. Pour the mixture in a thin stream into the egg mixture, whisking continuously. Return the mixture to the pan, reduce the heat to very low and continue whisking for 3–4 minutes until thickened slightly. Add the brioche pieces and simmer for a further 3–4 minutes until the brioche absorbs some of the custard.

3 Spoon the mixture into four 200ml/7fl oz/scant 1-cup ramekins and bake for 8–10 minutes until slightly puffed and just set. Serve with extra dulce de leche and cream for pouring over.

m'hanncha

The name of this Middle Eastern dessert translates as 'the snake' because of its coiled shape.

1 Preheat the oven to 200°C/400°F/Gas 6 and melt half of the butter in a small saucepan over a medium heat. Grease a large baking sheet with a little of the melted butter and set the rest aside. Put the unmelted butter, almonds, caster sugar, orange zest and orange flower water in a bowl, mix well and set aside.

2 Put 1 sheet of filo pastry on a work surface and keep the rest covered with a clean, damp tea towel while you work. Brush the pastry with some of the melted butter, then fold it in half, short end to short end, and brush again. Spoon one-quarter of the almond mixture along one of the long sides of the pastry, leaving a 1cm/½in border at both ends. Fold the short sides in towards the centre, then roll up the pastry from the almond end to enclose the mixture. Coil the pastry into a spiral and put it on the baking sheet, then brush generously with more melted butter. Repeat with the remaining pastry sheets, butter and filling.

3 Bake for 15 minutes, or until golden brown and crisp. Dust with icing sugar and serve hot.

115g/4oz butter, softened
85g/3oz/¾ cup ground almonds
2 tbsp caster sugar
finely grated zest of ½ large orange
1 tsp orange flower water
4 sheets of filo pastry
icing sugar, to serve

chocolate cream pots

Smooth and rich, this classic chocolate dessert is a favourite
with adults and children alike.

1 Put four 200ml/7fl oz/scant 1-cup ramekins or freezerproof
  glasses in the freezer to chill and fill a sink with about 10cm/4in
  iced water. Put the egg yolks, cornflour, caster sugar and
  4 tablespoons of the milk in a large heatproof bowl and whisk
  until combined, then set aside. Put the cream and the remaining
  milk in a saucepan and cook over a medium heat for 2 minutes
  until just boiling.
2 Pour the hot milk mixture into the egg mixture in a thin
  stream, whisking continuously. Return the mixture to the pan
  and continue whisking over a low heat for 5–6 minutes until
  thickened. Remove the pan from the heat, add the chocolate
  chips and vanilla extract and stir until the chocolate has melted.
3 Put the pan in the iced water and whisk for 5 minutes until
  cooled. Spoon the chocolate cream into the chilled ramekins and
  serve with crisp biscuits.

2 egg yolks
1 tbsp cornflour
4 tbsp caster sugar
200ml/7fl oz/scant 1 cup full-fat
  milk
200ml/7fl oz/scant 1 cup double
  cream
85g/3oz/1/2 cup dark chocolate
  chips
1/2 tsp vanilla extract
crisp biscuits, such as Langue
  de chat or shortbread, to serve

arroz con leches

Originating from Latin America, this simple dish of rice with milk
has become popular around the world.

1 Put the rice, both milks and the vanilla pod in a saucepan and
  bring to the boil over a medium heat, stirring occasionally. Reduce
  the heat to low and leave to simmer for 20 minutes, or until the
  rice is tender. Stir every 5 minutes to prevent the rice from
  sticking to the base of the pan. Remove from the heat.
2 Use the back of a knife to scrape out the seeds from the vanilla
  pod and add them back to the saucepan, then stir in the caster
  sugar to taste.
3 Divide the rice into four bowls, drizzle with the dulce de leche and
  and serve warm.

115g/4oz/1/2 cup risotto rice,
  such as arborio
170g/5oz tinned evaporated milk
455ml/16fl oz/scant 2 cups milk
1 vanilla pod, halved lengthways
2-3 tbsp caster sugar
4 tbsp dulce de leche or caramel
  sauce, to serve

butterscotch pudding

This unusual, delicious pudding comes from everyday ingredients.

3 eggs, separated
2 tbsp cornflour
250ml/9fl oz/1 cup milk
185g/6^1/$_2$oz/1 cup soft light
  brown sugar
85g/3oz butter
1 tsp vanilla extract
60g/2^1/$_4$oz/1^1/$_2$ cups fresh white
  breadcrumbs
a pinch of salt
4 tbsp caster sugar

1 Preheat the oven to 200°C/400°F/Gas 6. Whisk the egg yolks, cornflour and 3 tablespoons of the milk together in a large bowl and set aside. Put the brown sugar, butter and remaining milk in a saucepan and heat over a medium heat, stirring occasionally, for 2–3 minutes until the sugar has melted. Bring to the boil over a high heat, then remove from the heat and pour the mixture over the egg mixture in a thin stream, whisking continuously.

2 Return the mixture to the pan and continue whisking over a medium heat for 5–6 minutes until thickened. Remove from the heat and stir in the vanilla extract and breadcrumbs. Spoon the mixture into a 20cm/8in round, deep ovenproof dish and set aside.

3 Put the egg whites and salt in a large clean bowl and beat, using an electric mixer, until stiff peaks form. Whisk in the sugar in a thin stream until stiff and glossy and spoon the meringue over the butterscotch. Bake for 8–10 minutes until browned, then serve.

mochamallow mousses

Marshmallows help this egg-free mousse to set very quickly.

115g/4oz/2^1/$_2$ cups mini
  marshmallows
6 tablespoons hot coffee
100g/3^1/$_2$oz/^{1}/$_2$ cup dark chocolate
  chips
200ml/7fl oz/scant 1 cup double
  cream
^{1}/$_2$ tsp vanilla extract

Topping
2 tablespoons dark chocolate chips
4 tbsp double cream
1 chocolate muffin, cut into cubes
icing sugar, for dusting
chocolate curls (optional; see
  page 9), to decorate

1 Put four freezerproof glasses or bowls in the freezer to chill and fill a sink with 5cm/2in iced water. Put the marshmallows and coffee in a saucepan and cook over a low heat, stirring, for 3–4 minutes, until melted. Remove from the heat, add the chocolate chips and stir until melted. Put the pan in the iced water and leave to cool for 2 minutes, stirring.

2 Put the cream and vanilla in a large bowl and whip, using an electric mixer, until it just holds its shape. Add the cooled chocolate and whip for 1–2 minutes until thick. Spoon the mousse into the chilled glasses and freeze for 5–10 minutes until set.

3 Meanwhile, put the chocolate chips and cream for the topping in a heatproof bowl and rest it over a pan of gently simmering water, making sure the bottom of the bowl does not touch the water. Heat, stirring occasionally, for 2–3 minutes until the chocolate has melted. Top the mousses with the muffin pieces, then spoon the chocolate sauce over them and dust with icing sugar. Decorate with chocolate curls, if desired, and serve.

chocolate soufflés

These soufflés are rich, delicious and surprisingly easy to make.

1 Preheat the oven to 200°C/400°F/Gas 6 with a baking sheet inside. Put the chocolate chips and brandy in a heatproof bowl and rest it over a pan of gently simmering water, making sure the bottom of the bowl does not touch the water. Heat, stirring occasionally, for 2–3 minutes until the chocolate has melted, then remove the bowl from the heat and set aside to cool slightly.

2 Meanwhile, grease four 200ml/7fl oz/scant 1-cup ramekins with melted butter and dust the inside of each one with 1 teaspoon caster sugar. Stir the egg yolks into the cooled chocolate.

3 Put the egg whites and salt in a clean bowl and whisk, using an electric mixer, until stiff peaks form. Whisk in the caster sugar in a thin stream and continue whisking until the meringue is stiff and glossy. Stir one-quarter of the meringue into the chocolate to lighten it, then fold in the rest. Spoon the mixture into the ramekins and level by scraping a palette knife across the tops, removing any excess mixture. Bake on the baking sheet for 12–13 minutes until well risen. Dust with icing sugar and serve immediately.

115g/4oz/²/₃ cup dark chocolate chips
2 tbsp brandy
melted butter, for greasing
60g/2¹/₄oz/scant ¹/₃ cup caster sugar, plus 4 tsp for dusting
4 eggs, separated
a pinch of salt
icing sugar, for dusting

ice cream bites (see page 148)

CHAPTER SIX

30-minute desserts

With a full half an hour to devote to dessert, there's no reason why it can't be anything short of magnificent. For a taste of the Middle East, try moreish Baby Baklavas – their crisp layers of filo pastry and walnuts drenched in a sweet honey syrup will melt in your mouth. Apricot & Almond Crumble is a classic, comforting choice that's full of juicy fruit covered with a crunchy, nutty topping. And when it comes to perennial favourites, nothing beats hot Chocolate Fondant Puddings – their short baking time is a virtue, leaving a molten middle that mingles irresistibly with a cold and creamy accompaniment. These recipes are guaranteed to satisfy everyone's craving for something yummy.

apple & berry charlotte

Bread makes an easy and crisp topping for fruit and a nice alternative to a traditional pie or crumble.

2 eating apples, peeled, cored
    and cut into 1cm/^{1}/$_2$in chunks
150g/5^1/$_2$oz/1^1/$_2$ cups fresh
    or frozen berries, such as
    raspberries, blueberries
    and blackberries
75g/2^1/$_2$oz/^{1}/$_3$ cup caster sugar
40g/1^1/$_2$oz butter, softened
8 slices of slightly stale white
    bread, crusts removed
single cream, to serve

1 Preheat the oven to 200°C/400°F/Gas 6 with a baking sheet inside. Put the apples and berries in a 1l/35fl oz/4 cup baking dish and mix well. Set aside 1 tablespoon of the caster sugar and toss the rest with the apples and berries, then set aside.
2 Spread the butter thinly over one side of each slice of bread and cut the slices into triangles. Arrange the triangles over the fruit, buttered-sides up, and sprinkle with the reserved caster sugar.
3 Bake on the preheated baking sheet for 20-25 minutes until the bread is crisp and golden and the fruit is soft. Serve hot with cream.

tempura bananas with toffee sauce

A Japanese-inspired batter gives these banana fritters a crisp, light texture.

750ml/26fl oz/3 cups rapeseed oil,
    for deep-frying
55g/2oz/^{1}/$_2$ cup plain flour
2 tbsp cornflour
a pinch of salt
6 tbsp ice-cold sparkling water
3 large bananas, peeled and each
    cut into 4 chunks
1 tsp icing sugar, to serve

TOFFEE SAUCE:
100g/3^1/$_2$oz/scant ^{1}/$_2$ cup
    caster sugar
4 tbsp double cream

1 To make the sauce, put the caster sugar and 2 tablespoons water in a small saucepan and cook over a medium heat for 1-2 minutes, stirring occasionally, until the sugar has dissolved. Bring to the boil over a high heat and boil for 3-4 minutes until caramel in colour. Remove from the heat and carefully add the cream, stirring to dissolve any lumps, then set aside.
2 Heat the oil in a large deep saucepan or deep-fat fryer to 190°C/375°F. Put the flour, cornflour and salt in a bowl and stir in the sparkling water, using a fork, to make a thin batter.
3 Working in batches to avoid overcrowding the pan, dip the banana pieces in the batter and carefully put them in the oil. Fry for 2-3 minutes, turning regularly, until crisp and puffed. Remove from the oil, using a slotted spoon, and drain on kitchen paper.
4 Just before the fritters are done cooking, warm the toffee sauce over a low heat. Serve the bananas dusted with icing sugar and drizzled with the toffee sauce.

blueberry buckles

These cakes get their name because the fruit and topping tend to cause the cakes to 'buckle' rather than rise evenly.

1 Preheat the oven to 200°C/400°F/Gas 6 and generously butter four cups of a deep non-stick muffin tin. To make the topping, put the melted butter, plain flour, brown sugar and ginger in a bowl and stir until the mixture looks like large crumbs, then set aside.

2 Put the butter, caster sugar, egg, self-raising flour, vanilla extract and salt in another bowl and beat, using an electric mixer, until just combined, then fold in the blueberries. Spoon the mixture into the muffin cups and sprinkle with the topping.

3 Bake for 20 minutes until risen, golden and firm to the touch. Turn out the cakes and dust with icing sugar, then serve warm with whipped cream.

55g/2oz butter, softened, plus
    melted butter for greasing
4 tbsp caster sugar
1 egg
55g/2oz/$\frac{1}{2}$ cup self-raising flour
$\frac{1}{2}$ tsp vanilla extract
a pinch of salt
55g/2oz/$\frac{1}{3}$ cup blueberries
icing sugar, to decorate
whipped cream, to serve

TOPPING:
15g/$\frac{1}{2}$oz butter, melted
2 tbsp plain flour
1 tbsp soft light brown sugar
$\frac{1}{4}$ tsp ground ginger

rhubarb crumble

Partially cooking the rhubarb at the beginning of this recipe substantially reduces this crumble's time in the oven.

1 Preheat the oven to 200°C/400°F/Gas 6 with a baking sheet inside. Put the rhubarb, caster sugar and orange zest in a large frying pan and cook over a medium heat, stirring occasionally, for 5 minutes or until the juices start to run and the sugar has dissolved.

2 Meanwhile, to make the crumble topping, put the flour, butter and ginger, if using, in a food processor and blend for 1 minute, or until the mixture resembles breadcrumbs. Add the brown sugar and pulse 2–3 times to combine.

3 Spoon the rhubarb into a deep 20cm/8in ovenproof serving dish and sprinkle with the crumble topping. Bake on the preheated baking sheet for 20 minutes, or until the topping is brown and the filling is bubbling. Serve hot with cream.

600g/1lb 5oz rhubarb, cut into
    2.5cm/$\frac{1}{2}$in pieces
85g/3oz/$\frac{1}{3}$ cup caster sugar
finely grated zest of
    1 large orange

CRUMBLE TOPPING:
170g/6oz/1$\frac{1}{2}$ cups plain flour
40g/1$\frac{1}{2}$oz butter,
    cut into large cubes
1 tsp ground ginger (optional)
75g/2$\frac{1}{2}$oz/$\frac{1}{3}$ cup soft light
    brown sugar
single cream or vanilla ice cream,
    to serve

plum & walnut torte

Ground walnuts give this cake a wonderful taste and texture.

115g/4oz butter, softened, plus
    extra for greasing
680g/1lb 8oz red plums, halved,
    pitted and each half halved again
200g/7oz/³⁄₄ cup plus 2 tbsp
    caster sugar
55g/2oz/scant ¹⁄₂ cup chopped
    walnuts
2 eggs
¹⁄₂ tsp vanilla extract
115g/4oz/³⁄₄ cup plus 2 tbsp
    self-raising flour
icing sugar, to decorate

1 Preheat the oven to 200°C/400°F/Gas 6. Grease a 20cm/8in round cake tin with butter and line the base with baking parchment cut to fit. Put the plums, cut-sides up, in two baking dishes and sprinkle with 85g/3oz/¹⁄₃ cup of the caster sugar.

2 Put the walnuts in a food processor and blend until finely ground. Add the butter, eggs, vanilla extract, flour and remaining caster sugar and pulse until just combined. Scrape the mixture into the cake tin and level the surface. Put the plums on the lower shelf of the oven and the cake on the middle shelf. Bake for 20 minutes or until the plums are slightly softened and the cake is brown and firm to the touch. Remove the cake and plums from the oven and leave to cool for 2–3 minutes.

3 Carefully turn the cake out on to a plate. Peel off the parchment and arrange the plums on top. Dust with icing sugar and serve.

dutch apple pancake

This pancake is baked in the oven rather than fried, so it's puffy and light.

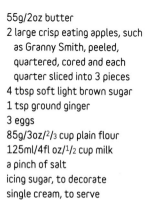

55g/2oz butter
2 large crisp eating apples, such
    as Granny Smith, peeled,
    quartered, cored and each
    quarter sliced into 3 pieces
4 tbsp soft light brown sugar
1 tsp ground ginger
3 eggs
85g/3oz/²⁄₃ cup plain flour
125ml/4fl oz/¹⁄₂ cup milk
a pinch of salt
icing sugar, to decorate
single cream, to serve

1 Preheat the oven to 230°C/450°F/Gas 8. Melt the butter in a large heavy-based, ovenproof frying pan over a medium heat. When it is foaming, add the apples, brown sugar and ginger and cook, stirring occasionally, for 5 minutes until the sugar has dissolved and the apples have softened slightly.

2 Meanwhile, put the eggs, flour, milk and salt in a blender and blend for 1–2 minutes until smooth. Pour the mixture into the pan and immediately transfer to the oven. Bake for 10 minutes, then lower the oven temperature to 200°C/400°F/Gas 6 and bake for a further 10 minutes until puffed up and golden.

3 Remove from the oven and dust with icing sugar. Cut and serve the pancake from the pan and drizzle with cream.

apricot & almond crumble

Crumbles can take a long time to bake, but using a very soft fruit, such as apricots, speeds up the time considerably.

1 Preheat the oven to 200°C/400°F/Gas 6 with a baking sheet inside. Put the apricots in a 20cm/8in ovenproof serving dish and sprinkle with 2 tablespoons of the caster sugar, then set aside.

2 Put the almonds in a food processor and blend until roughly chopped. Add the flour and butter and blend again until the mixture resembles breadcrumbs. Add the remaining caster sugar and pulse to combine. Scatter the mixture over the apricots.

3 Bake on the preheated baking sheet for 20–25 minutes until the filling is bubbling and the topping is crisp and golden brown. Spoon into four bowls and serve hot with ice cream.

900g/2lb apricots, halved, pitted and each half halved again
100g/3¹/2oz/scant ¹/2 cup caster sugar
55g/2oz/¹/3 cup blanched almonds
115g/4oz/scant 1 cup plain flour
40g/1¹/2oz cold butter
vanilla ice cream or single cream, to serve

banana tarte tatins

Bananas cook quickly and make an interesting, unexpected topping for a tarte tatin, replacing the more usual apples.

1 Preheat the oven to 220°C/425°F/Gas 7 and line a baking sheet with foil. Grease four 7.5cm/3in loose-bottomed tart tins with melted butter and line the bases with baking parchment circles cut to fit. Sprinkle the caster sugar over the base of the tins.

2 Put the bananas in the tins, cut-sides up, trimming to fit as necessary. Cut out four rounds from the puff pastry, using a 9cm/3¹/2in biscuit cutter, and cover the bananas, tucking the edges of the pastry into the tins. Put the tins on the baking sheet and bake for 13–14 minutes until the pastry is risen, golden and crisp.

3 Remove the baking sheet from the oven and cover with a large chopping board. Using oven mitts or folded tea towels, carefully invert the baking sheet to drop the tarts on to the chopping board. Peel away the foil and carefully lift off the tins, bases and baking parchment, repositioning any loose pieces of banana with the tip of a knife. Transfer the tarts to four plates and serve with cream.

melted butter, for greasing
2 tbsp caster sugar
3 slightly underripe bananas, peeled and halved lengthways
1 sheet of ready-rolled puff pastry, about 250g/9oz
single cream, to serve

spiced caramel kumquat compôte

Kumquats, with their sweet rind and tart fruit, make a colourful winter compôte.

300g/10^1/$_2$oz/1^1/$_2$ cups caster sugar
450g/1lb kumquats, each sliced into 4 pieces crossways
2 star anise
2 small cinnamon sticks
5 whole black peppercorns
500ml/17fl oz/2 cups vanilla ice cream

1 Put the sugar and 4 tablespoons water in a saucepan and cook, stirring, over a medium heat for 2–3 minutes until the sugar has dissolved. Bring to the boil over a high heat and boil for 4–5 minutes, swirling the pan occasionally, until the sugar turns a caramel colour.

2 Remove from the heat and carefully pour in 150ml/5fl oz/scant ^{2}/$_3$ cup water. Protect your hand, as the caramel may splutter.

3 Return the caramel to a low heat and add the kumquats, star anise, cinnamon and peppercorns. Cook, stirring, until any traces of hard caramel have dissolved.

4 Bring to the boil again, then reduce the heat to low and simmer for 15 minutes until the kumquats are tender. Shortly before serving, remove the ice cream from the freezer and leave to stand at room temperature to soften slightly. Serve the warm kumquat over the ice cream.

rustic apple pie

Free-formed fruit pies are quick to make and have a rustic charm that's welcomed at the end of a meal.

1 sheet of ready-rolled shortcrust pastry, about 225g/8oz
2 large eating apples, peeled, cored and sliced
2 tbsp caster sugar
^{1}/$_4$ tsp cinnamon (optional)
1 egg, beaten
icing sugar, to serve
ice cream or whipped cream, to serve

1 Preheat the oven to 200°C/400°F/Gas 6 and line a baking sheet with baking parchment. Cut out a rough 27cm/11in round from the pastry and put it on the baking sheet.

2 Put the apples on the pastry, heaping them up slightly towards the centre and leaving a 4cm/1^1/$_2$in-wide border of pastry around the edge. Sprinkle with the caster sugar and cinnamon, if using. Bring the border of the pastry inwards over the apples, pleating and folding as you go so it lies flat over the edge of the apples. Brush the pastry with the egg.

3 Bake for 20 minutes, or until the pastry is golden brown and the apples have softened slightly. Dust with icing sugar and serve hot with ice cream.

ginger & apricot baked apples

Cutting the apples in half speeds up their time in the oven, so dessert gets to the table faster.

1 Preheat the oven to 200°C/400°F/Gas 6 and grease a baking dish large enough to hold the apple halves upright with butter. Put the apples in the dish, cut-sides up. Put the apricots, sugar and preserved and ground ginger in a small bowl and mix well, then pack this mixture into the centre of the apple halves, where the cores used to be. Divide the butter over the tops of the apple halves.

2 Fill the dish 5mm/$^1/_4$in deep with water. Bake for 10 minutes, then baste by spooning the juices in the dish over the apples.

3 Bake for a further 15 minutes, or until the apples are soft. Check occasionally and add a splash of water if the dish becomes too dry. Carefully transfer the apples to bowls and spoon any juices from the baking dish over the top. Serve hot with cream.

30g/1oz butter, cut into 4 pieces, plus extra for greasing
4 floury-type eating apples, such as Spartan or Macintosh, halved crossways and cored
8 dried apricots, chopped
2 tbsp soft light brown sugar
2 tsp chopped preserved or crystallized ginger
$^1/_4$ tsp ground ginger
single cream, to serve

sticky toffee puddings

Baking individual puddings makes this dessert elegant enough to be served at even the smartest dinner parties.

1 Preheat the oven to 200°C/400°F/Gas 6 and generously butter four 200ml/7fl oz/scant 1-cup pudding basins or ramekins. Put half of the butter in a bowl and add the caster sugar, flour, egg, vanilla extract and salt. Beat, using an electric mixer, until just combined, then stir in the dates and walnuts. Spoon the mixture into the pudding basins and bake for 20–22 minutes until risen, golden and firm.

2 Shortly before the puddings are done baking, put the brown sugar, cream and remaining butter in a saucepan and cook over a low heat, stirring continuously, until the sugar has dissolved. Bring to the boil and cook over a high heat, stirring, for 1 minute, then set aside.

3 Carefully unmould each pudding on to a plate, right-side up. Spoon over the warm sauce and serve with extra cream for pouring over.

115g/4oz butter, softened, plus extra for greasing
4 tbsp caster sugar
55g/2oz/$^1/_2$ cup self-raising flour
1 egg
$^1/_2$ tsp vanilla extract
a pinch of salt
4 pitted dates, roughly chopped
2 tbsp chopped walnuts
100g/3$^1/_2$oz/$^1/_2$ cup soft light brown sugar
100ml/3$^1/_2$fl oz/scant $^1/_2$ cup double cream, plus extra for serving

peach galette

A puff-pastry tart case makes an impressive container
for sweet summer peaches.

1 sheet of ready-rolled puff
    pastry, about 250g/9oz
2 large peaches, halved, pitted
    and very thinly sliced
1 tbsp vanilla sugar (see page 40)
    or caster sugar
1 egg, beaten
2 tbsp apricot jam
whipped cream or vanilla ice
    cream, to serve

1 Preheat the oven to 220°C/425°F/Gas 7 and line a large baking
   sheet with baking parchment. Put the pastry on the baking sheet
   and mark a 1cm/^{1}/$_2$in-wide border all round it, using a sharp knife,
   then prick inside the border, using a fork. Spread the peach slices
   over the pastry, keeping them inside the border. Sprinkle the
   sugar over the peaches, then brush the border of the pastry
   with the egg.

2 Bake for 15 minutes, or until the pastry is golden underneath and
   puffed at the edges. Meanwhile, put the jam in a small saucepan
   and heat over a low heat, stirring, for 1–2 minutes until runny.

3 Remove the galette from the oven and slide it on to a serving
   plate. Brush the peaches with the warm jam, then slice and serve
   with whipped cream.

lemon surprise puddings

The surprise when you dig into these puddings is a zesty lemon
curd on the base.

30g/1oz butter, softened, plus
    extra for greasing
1 egg, separated, plus 1 egg white
a large pinch of salt
100g/3^1/$_2$oz/scant ^{1}/$_2$ cup caster
    sugar
juice and finely grated zest
    of 1 lemon
2 tbsp milk
55g/2oz/^{1}/$_2$ cup plain flour
single cream, to serve

1 Preheat the oven to 200°C/400°F/Gas 6 and bring a kettle of
   water to the boil. Grease four 200ml/7fl oz/scant 1-cup ramekins
   with butter and put them in a small roasting tin. Put the egg
   whites and salt in a large clean bowl and beat, using an electric
   mixer, until stiff peaks form, then set aside.

2 In a separate bowl, use the mixer (no need to wash the beaters)
   to beat together the egg yolk, butter, caster sugar, lemon juice
   and zest, milk and flour until just combined (it may look a little
   curdled). Stir in one-quarter of the egg whites to loosen, then
   fold in the remaining egg whites and spoon the mixture into
   the ramekins.

3 Put the ramekins in the tin and add enough boiling water to the
   tin to come half-way up the sides of the ramekins. Bake for
   17–20 minutes, or until risen and just firm to the touch. Serve
   hot with cream.

apple spice cakes

Warm, dense apple cake is a delicious autumnal dessert, and these muffin-sized ones make delightful individual treats.

115g/4oz/scant 1 cup
    self-raising flour
1/4 tsp bicarbonate of soda
1 tsp mixed spice
1/2 tsp ground ginger
a large pinch of salt
115g/4oz butter, softened
115g/4oz/heaped 1/2 cup soft
    light brown sugar
2 eggs
1/2 tsp vanilla extract
1 tbsp natural yogurt
1 eating apple, grated
85g/3oz/2/3 cup raisins
1 tbsp demerara sugar
vanilla ice cream or whipped
    cream, to serve

1 Preheat the oven to 190°C/375°F/Gas 5 and line 8 cups of a muffin tin with paper cupcake cases. Sift the flour, bicarbonate of soda, mixed spice, ginger and salt into a large bowl. Add the butter, brown sugar, eggs, vanilla extract and yogurt and beat, using an electric mixer, until just combined. Fold in the apple and raisins.
2 Spoon the mixture into the paper cases and sprinkle with the demerara sugar. Bake for 20 minutes, or until firm to the touch.
3 Carefully remove the cakes from the tin and set aside to cool for 1–2 minutes, then peel the papers off. Serve with ice cream.

pear & almond puddings

This variation on Eve's pudding is bursting with ripe fruit and makes a lovely, comforting dessert.

55g/2oz butter, softened, plus
    extra for greasing
2 large, ripe pears, peeled,
    quartered and cored, then each
    quarter quartered again
75g/21/2oz/1/3 cup caster sugar
1 egg
30g/1oz/1/4 cup self-raising flour
30g/1oz/1/4 cup ground almonds
3 drops of almond extract
1 tbsp flaked almonds (optional)
single cream or vanilla ice cream,
    to serve

1 Preheat the oven to 200°C/400°F/Gas 6 and grease four 200ml/7fl oz/scant 1-cup ramekins with butter. Put the pears in the ramekins and sprinkle 1 tablespoon of the caster sugar over each one.
2 Put the butter, egg, flour, almonds, almond extract and remaining caster sugar in a large bowl and beat, using an electric mixer, until just combined. Spoon the mixture over the pears, then sprinkle with the flaked almonds, if using.
3 Put the ramekins on a baking sheet and bake for 20 minutes, or until the sponge is risen, golden and firm to the touch. Serve hot with cream.

raspberry sponge drops

Made with a sponge cake mixture but dropped free-form on to baking sheets, these can be stacked to make lovely towers layered with cream and berries.

1 Preheat the oven to 180°C/350°F/Gas 4 and line two baking sheets with baking parchment. Put the butter, caster sugar, flour, egg, vanilla extract and salt in a bowl and beat, using an electric mixer, for 2–3 minutes until just combined.

2 Drop 12 tablespoonfuls of the mixture on to the baking sheets, spacing well apart. Bake for 10–12 minutes until golden and firm to the touch. Carefully slide the parchment and sponge drops on to wire racks and leave to cool for 5 minutes.

3 Meanwhile, put the cream and icing sugar in a bowl and whip, using an electric mixer, until stiff peaks form. Put 1 sponge drop on each of four plates and divide half the whipped cream over them. Nestle half of the raspberries into the cream and then layer again. Top with the remaining sponge drops and serve dusted with icing sugar.

55g/2oz butter, softened
4 tbsp caster sugar
55g/2oz/$\frac{1}{2}$ cup self-raising flour
1 egg
$\frac{1}{4}$ tsp vanilla extract
a pinch of salt
250ml/9fl oz/1 cup double cream
1 tsp icing sugar, plus extra
 to serve
175g/6oz/heaped 1$\frac{1}{3}$ cups
 raspberries

blueberry pie

Blueberries are a perfect summer pie filling, and using frozen ones means you can enjoy this all-American treat all year round.

1 Preheat the oven to 225°C/425°F/Gas 7 with a baking sheet inside. Put the blueberries and cornflour in a bowl and toss well. Set aside 1 tablespoon of the caster sugar and stir the rest into the blueberries. Put the blueberries in a 20cm/8in pie dish and brush the edge of the dish with a little of the egg.

2 Lay the pastry over the dish and press on to the edge of the pie dish to secure. Trim away any excess pastry, using a sharp knife, then press the edges of the crust with a fork to seal. Brush the crust with the egg, sprinkle with the remaining caster sugar and cut a small steam hole in the centre.

3 Bake on the preheated baking sheet for 20 minutes, or until the crust is golden brown. Serve hot with ice cream.

450g/1lb/3 cups fresh or frozen
 blueberries
2 tbsp cornflour
75g/2^1/$_2$oz/^{1}/$_3$ cup caster sugar
1 egg, beaten
1 sheet of ready-rolled shortcrust
 pastry, about 225g/8oz
vanilla ice cream or whipped cream,
 to serve

hot chocolate, raisin & rum pudding

The liquid poured over the top of this pudding transforms during baking into a rich sauce sitting under a chocolate sponge.

1 Preheat the oven to 200°C/400°F/Gas 6 with a baking sheet inside and grease a deep 20cm/8in ovenproof serving dish with oil. Put the brown sugar, rum, 2 tablespoons of the cocoa powder and 150ml/5fl oz/scant ^{2}/$_3$ cup water in a small saucepan and heat over a medium heat for 2–3 minutes, whisking occasionally, until the sugar has dissolved.

2 Meanwhile, put the chocolate chips, flour, caster sugar and remaining cocoa powder in a food processor and blend for 1 minute until the chocolate is finely chopped. Add the egg, oil and milk and blend for 1 minute until well mixed, then add the raisins and pulse 1–2 times to combine.

3 Pour the chocolate mixture into the dish, then spoon the rum mixture over the top. Bake on the preheated baking sheet for 20 minutes, or until risen and firm to the touch and a sauce has formed underneath the sponge. Serve hot with cream.

3 tbsp sunflower oil, plus extra
 for greasing
100g/3^1/$_2$oz/^{1}/$_2$ cup soft light
 brown sugar
4 tbsp dark rum
40g/1^1/$_2$oz/^{1}/$_3$ cup cocoa powder
100g/3^1/$_2$oz/scant ^{2}/$_3$ cup dark
 chocolate chips
200g/7oz/scant 1^2/$_3$ cups
 self-raising flour
200g/7oz/1 cup caster sugar
1 egg
185ml/6fl oz/^{3}/$_4$ cup milk
4 tbsp raisins
single cream, to serve

▶ice cream bites

Small bites of chocolate and ice cream are a great way to finish a meal. These can be served as dessert, or with coffee if you're really in a hurry and want to skip the dessert course.

200g/7oz/scant 1¼ cups dark chocolate chips
250ml/9fl oz/1 cup strawberry ice cream
2 small strawberries, thinly sliced, to decorate

1 Put the chocolate chips in a heatproof bowl and rest it over a pan of gently simmering water, making sure the bottom of the bowl does not touch the water. Heat, stirring occasionally, for 2–3 minutes, until the chocolate has melted. Remove the bowl from the heat and set aside to cool slightly.

2 Meanwhile, line a mini muffin tin that will fit in your freezer with 8 mini paper cupcake cases. Spoon some of the chocolate into the base of each one and spread it up the sides of the case, using the back of a teaspoon. Put the tin in the freezer for 5 minutes, or until the chocolate has become firm, then apply a second layer of chocolate and return to the freezer for a further 5 minutes, or until firm. Meanwhile, remove the ice cream from the freezer and leave to stand at room temperature to soften slightly.

3 Remove the paper cases from the tin and gently peel the paper away. If necessary, warm the outside of the cups slightly with your hands to help the paper peel away. Using a melon baller, scoop 1 small ball of ice cream into each of the chocolate cups, decorate with a slice of strawberry and serve immediately.

sticky sponge pudding

This pudding may be reminiscent of schooldays, but it's still a favourite with adults and children alike – for good reason.

115g/4oz butter, softened, plus extra for greasing
200ml/7fl oz/scant 1 cup golden syrup
115g/4oz/½ cup caster sugar
115g/4oz/scant 1 cup self-raising flour
1 egg, beaten
½ tsp vanilla extract
½ tsp ground ginger
a pinch of salt
single cream, to serve

1 Preheat the oven to 200°C/400°F/Gas 6 and generously grease a 20cm/8in ovenproof serving dish with butter. Pour half of the golden syrup into the dish and set aside.

2 Put the butter and caster sugar in a large bowl and beat, using an electric mixer, for 1–2 minutes until fluffy. Add the flour, egg, vanilla extract, ginger and salt and beat until just combined. Spoon the mixture into the dish and bake for 20–25 minutes until the sponge is risen, golden and just firm to the touch.

3 Meanwhile, warm the remaining golden syrup in a small pan over a low heat. Serve the sponge with the extra syrup and cream.

baby baklavas

Baklava can be complicated to make, so instead, try this easy version, which looks as good as it tastes.

40g/1¹/₂oz butter, melted, plus
    extra for greasing
4 sheets of filo pastry
60g/2¹/₄oz/¹/₂ cup walnuts,
    finely chopped
100ml/3¹/₂fl oz/scant ¹/₂ cup clear
    honey
Greek yogurt, to serve
2 tablespoons chopped pistachios

1 Preheat the oven to 200°C/400°F/Gas 6 and grease a large baking sheet with some of the melted butter. Put 1 sheet of filo pastry on the baking sheet and keep the rest covered with a clean, damp tea towel while you work. Brush with butter, trim any overhanging pastry, then repeat with a second layer of filo. Scatter half of the walnuts over the pastry and cover with the remaining sheets of filo, brushing with butter between each layer and trimming any overhanging pastry. Bake for 8–10 minutes, until golden and crisp. Meanwhile, warm the honey and 2 tablespoons water in a small saucepan over a low heat.

2 Slide the baklava on to a chopping board and leave to cool for 2 minutes, then cut the baklava into 8 rectangles, using a large, sharp knife. Cut each rectangle in half diagonally to make triangles and stack them on a serving plate, drizzling a little of the honey syrup between each layer. Sprinkle with the pistachios, then serve with yogurt and any remaining honey sauce.

easy carrot halwa

This rich, simple version of the popular Indian dessert is delicious served warm with ice cream.

1 Put the carrots, both milks, brown sugar and ginger in a large frying pan or wok and cook over a medium heat, stirring, for 2–3 minutes until the sugar has dissolved. Bring to the boil over a high heat and boil, uncovered, for 10 minutes, stirring occasionally.
2 Add the butter, reduce the heat to low and simmer, uncovered, for a further 10 minutes, or until the liquid has been absorbed and the carrot has turned a deep golden colour.
3 Remove from the heat, stir in the raisins, almonds and pistachios and leave to stand for 5 minutes, then spoon the halwa into four bowls and serve with ice cream.

450g/1lb carrots, peeled and coarsely grated
400ml/14fl oz tinned condensed milk
125ml/4^1/2fl oz/^{1}/2 cup full-fat milk
55g/2oz/^{1}/4 cup soft light brown sugar
^{1}/2 tsp ground ginger
30g/1oz butter
4 tbsp raisins
4 tbsp flaked almonds
4 tbsp unsalted pistachios, chopped
vanilla ice cream, to serve

ginger puddings with white chocolate sauce

Sticky, spicy ginger puddings with a vanilla-scented sauce make a comforting dessert for a cold winter's evening.

1 Preheat the oven to 200°C/400°F/Gas 6 and generously butter four 200ml/7fl oz/scant 1-cup pudding moulds or ramekins. Put the butter, brown sugar and treacle in a small saucepan and cook over a medium heat, stirring, for 2–3 minutes until the sugar has dissolved and the butter has melted. Remove from the heat, add the milk, flour, ground ginger, bicarbonate of soda and 1 egg yolk and whisk until smooth.
2 Divide the mixture into the moulds; they will be about half full. Bake for 20 minutes, or until the cakes are firm on top and shrinking away from the side of the moulds. Leave to cool for 5 minutes, then unmould on to four plates and sprinkle with the chopped ginger.
3 Meanwhile, put the remaining egg yolk, cornflour, caster sugar and cream in a small saucepan and cook over a low heat, whisking continuously, for 5 minutes until smooth and thickened. Remove from the heat, add the chocolate chips and stir until melted. Serve the puddings with the sauce.

55g/2oz butter, softened, plus extra for greasing
55g/2oz/^{1}/4 cup soft light brown sugar
3 tbsp treacle
80ml/2^1/2fl oz/^{1}/3 cup milk
40g/1^1/2oz/^{1}/3 cup plain flour
1 tsp ground ginger
^{1}/2 tsp bicarbonate of soda
2 egg yolks
1 tsp chopped preserved or crystallized ginger
^{1}/2 tbsp cornflour
^{1}/2 tbsp caster sugar
150ml/5^1/2fl oz/scant ^{2}/3 cup double cream
4 tbsp white chocolate chips

chocolate croissant puddings

This is a clever way to turn a breakfast favourite into an outstanding dessert.

2 chocolate croissants, torn into bite-sized pieces
200ml/7fl oz/scant 1 cup milk
200ml/7fl oz/scant 1 cup double cream
2 egg yolks
2 tbsp caster sugar
1 tbsp cornflour
1/4 tsp vanilla extract
icing sugar, to serve

1 Preheat the oven to 180°C/350°F/Gas 4 and bring a kettle of water to the boil. Divide the croissant pieces into four 200ml/ 7fl oz/scant 1-cup ramekins and put the ramekins in a small roasting tin. Put the milk and cream in a large saucepan and bring just to boiling over a medium heat, then set aside.

2 Put the egg yolks, caster sugar, cornflour and vanilla extract in a bowl and whisk together, then whisk in the hot milk mixture in a thin stream. Return the mixture to the saucepan and cook over a medium heat, whisking continuously, for 2–3 minutes until slightly thickened. Pour the custard into the ramekins.

3 Pour enough boiling water into the roasting tin to come half way up the sides of the ramekins. Bake for 20 minutes, or until the custard has just set. Remove the ramekins from the water, dust the tops with a little icing sugar and serve hot.

▶ chocolate fondant puddings

These classic chocolate puddings have irresistible melting centres.

115g/4oz butter, plus extra for greasing
100g/3 1/2oz/scant 2/3 cup dark chocolate chips
2 eggs, plus 2 egg yolks
4 tbsp caster sugar
1/2 tsp vanilla extract
a pinch of salt
2 tbsp plain flour
1 tbsp cocoa powder
vanilla ice cream, to serve
raspberries, to serve

1 Preheat the oven to 190°C/375°F/Gas 5 and generously grease four 200ml/7fl oz/scant 1-cup pudding moulds with butter. Put the chocolate chips and butter in a heatproof bowl and rest it over a pan of gently simmering water, making sure the bottom of the bowl does not touch the water. Heat, stirring occasionally, for 4–5 minutes until melted. Remove the bowl from the heat.

2 Put the eggs, egg yolks, caster sugar, vanilla extract and salt in a large bowl and beat, using an electric mixer, for 4–5 minutes until the mixture is pale, mousse-like and three times its original volume. Drizzle the chocolate mixture into the bowl and sift in the flour and cocoa, then fold together until just combined.

3 Spoon the mixture into the moulds and put them on a baking sheet. Bake for 10 minutes, or until just set on top. Remove from the oven and leave to stand for 1 minute, then turn them out on to four plates and serve immediately with ice cream and berries.

peanut butter pie

Peanut butter pie is an American diner classic that will satisfy anyone with a sweet tooth.

200g/7oz digestive biscuits
85g/3oz butter
100g/3^1/$_2$oz/scant ^{2}/$_3$ cup dark chocolate chips
225g/8oz/1 cup cream cheese
200g/7oz/scant 1 cup smooth peanut butter
55g/2oz/scant ^{1}/$_2$ cup icing sugar
125ml/4fl oz/^{1}/$_2$ cup double cream
1 large banana, peeled and sliced, to serve
30g/1oz milk chocolate, to decorate

1 Put the biscuits in a plastic bag and crush to fine crumbs, using a rolling pin, then set aside. Melt the butter and chocolate chips in a small saucepan over a very low heat, stirring occasionally. Add the crumbs and stir until well coated in the chocolate mixture. Press the crumbs firmly into the base of a 20cm/8in loose-bottomed tart tin and freeze for 5 minutes.

2 Meanwhile, put the cream cheese, peanut butter and icing sugar in a bowl and beat, using an electric mixer, for 1–2 minutes until smooth. Add the cream and beat again until combined.

3 Spoon the filling into the crumb base and return the pie to the freezer for a further 15 minutes.

4 Carefully remove the outer ring of the tart tin and transfer the pie to a serving plate. Peel and slice the banana and arrange the pieces around the edge, then grate the chocolate over the pie. Serve immediately.

chocolate-mint mousses

Traditional dark chocolate mousse is spiked with refreshing mint.

115g/4oz/^{2}/$_3$ cup dark chocolate chips
4 eggs, separated
^{1}/$_4$ tsp peppermint extract
2 tbsp caster sugar
chocolate-coated mint wafers, to decorate
mint sprigs, to decorate

1 Put four freezerproof glasses or bowls in the freezer to chill. Put the chocolate chips in a large heatproof bowl and rest it over a pan of gently simmering water, making sure the bottom of the bowl does not touch the water. Heat, stirring occasionally, for 2–3 minutes until the chocolate has melted. Remove the bowl from the heat and set aside to cool slightly.

2 Beat the egg yolks and peppermint extract together, then stir this mixture into the chocolate and set aside. Put the egg whites in a clean bowl and whisk, using an electric mixer, until stiff peaks form. Whisk in the caster sugar in a thin stream and continue whisking until the meringue is stiff and glossy.

3 Stir one-quarter of the meringue into the chocolate mixture to lighten, then fold in the rest. Spoon the mousse into the chilled glasses and return to the freezer for 10 minutes. Serve decorated with chocolate-coated mint wafers and mint sprigs.

cinnamon-sugared churros

Spaniards love these light doughnuts for breakfast, but they are just as delicious served for dessert.

1 Heat the oil in a deep heavy-based saucepan or deep-fat fryer to 180°C/350°F. Preheat the oven to 70°C/150°F/Gas 1/4. Put the butter, salt and 250ml/9fl oz/1 cup water in a saucepan and heat over a medium heat, stirring, until the butter has melted. Bring to the boil and boil for 1 minute, then remove from the heat, add the flour and beat with a wooden spoon until a ball of dough forms. Transfer the dough to a bowl and leave to cool for 5 minutes.

2 Beat the eggs into the dough, one at a time, with the wooden spoon, until a thick mixture forms. Spoon the mixture into a pastry bag fitted with a 1cm/1/2in star nozzle. Mix the icing sugar and cinnamon together in a bowl and set aside.

3 Working in batches to avoid overcrowding the pan, squeeze 10cm/4in strips of batter into the hot oil and fry for 4 minutes, turning regularly, until golden. Remove from the oil, using a slotted spoon, and drain on kitchen paper. Keep warm in the oven while you fry the rest. Dust with the cinnamon sugar and serve hot.

750ml/26fl oz/3 cups rapeseed oil, for deep-frying
115g/4oz butter, diced
1/4 tsp salt
115g/4oz/scant 1 cup plain flour
3 eggs
2 tbsp icing sugar
1/4 tsp cinnamon

thai forbidden rice pudding

The black 'forbidden' rice in this Thai favourite turns a deep purple colour when cooked, making a stunning presentation.

1 Put the rice, vanilla pod, coconut milk and milk in a large heavy-based saucepan and bring to the boil over a high heat. Reduce the heat to medium and simmer for 25 minutes, stirring occasionally and adding extra milk, if needed.

2 Meanwhile, put the sesame seeds in a dry frying pan and cook over a medium heat, stirring frequently, for 2–3 minutes until golden and fragrant. Immediately transfer to a plate to cool.

3 Remove the vanilla pod from the rice and scrape out the seeds into the rice. Add the caster sugar and stir well, then divide the rice into bowls. Top with whipped cream and sprinkle with the sesame seeds. Serve hot with extra sugar for stirring in, if desired.

200g/7oz/heaped 1 cup black forbidden rice
1 vanilla pod, halved
400ml/14fl oz/1 2/3 cups coconut milk
300ml/10 1/2fl oz/scant 1 1/4 cups milk, plus extra if needed
1 tbsp sesame seeds
2 tbsp caster sugar, plus extra (optional) to serve
whipped cream, to serve

▶ warm chocolate roulade

This chocolate roulade, made with a thin sponge, bakes quickly, so it can be on the table in less time than you might imagine.

3 eggs, at room temperature
1/2 tsp vanilla extract
100g/31/2oz/scant 1/2 cup caster
  sugar
30g/1oz/1/3 cup cocoa powder
55g/2oz/scant 1/2 cup plain flour
6 tbsp raspberry jam
1 tbsp icing sugar, for dusting
raspberries, to serve
whipped cream (optional), to serve

1 Preheat the oven to 180°C/350°F/Gas 4 and line a 32 x 23cm/ 13 x 9in Swiss roll tin with baking parchment, leaving some parchment hanging over the edges of the tin. Put the eggs and vanilla extract in a large bowl. Set aside 1 tablespoon of the caster sugar and add the rest to the eggs. Beat, using an electric mixer, for 4–5 minutes until the mixture is pale, mousse-like and about four times its original volume.

2 Sift the cocoa and flour into the egg mixture and fold in. Spoon the cake mixture into the tin and gently spread it out, levelling the surface. Bake for 10–12 minutes until risen and firm to the touch.

3 Meanwhile, put a large piece of baking parchment on a work surface and sprinkle it with the reserved caster sugar. Put the jam in a small saucepan and heat over a low heat, stirring, for 1–2 minutes until runny. Turn out the cake on to the parchment, spread the jam over it and gently roll up from one of the short ends, using the parchment as a guide. Dust with icing sugar, then slice and serve with raspberries and whipped cream, if desired.

ricotta beignets

Ricotta makes these fritters as light as a cloud.

500ml/17fl oz/2 cups rapeseed oil,
  for deep-frying
4 tbsp clear honey
300g/101/2oz/scant 11/4 cups
  ricotta cheese
2 eggs
2 tbsp caster sugar
1 tsp vanilla extract
85g/3oz/2/3 cup self-raising flour
icing sugar, to serve

1 Heat the oil in a large heavy-based saucepan or deep-fat fryer to 180°C/350°F and line a plate with several layers of kitchen paper. Put the honey and 1 tablespoon water in a small saucepan and cook over a low heat, stirring, until bubbling, then set aside.

2 Put the ricotta in a large bowl and beat in the eggs, caster sugar and vanilla extract, using an electric mixer, then fold in the flour. Working in batches, drop 3 rounded tablespoons of the mixture into the hot oil and fry for 2–3 minutes, turning often, until golden brown and slightly puffed. Remove from the oil, using a slotted spoon, and drain on kitchen paper.

3 Dust the beignets with icing sugar and drizzle with the honey. Serve immediately.

index

index

index